To. Roger...

Julia. G.D. TULLEY
11/2/015.

First published in the UK by Gibson Publishing

Once Upon a Spook
Text copyright © 2013 by Gary Tulley
Image copyright © 2013 by Gary Tulley

A CIP catalogue record for this title is available from the British Library.
All rights reserved. No part of this publication may be reproduced, stored in a retrieval system, or transmitted in any form or by any means, electronic, mechanical, photocopying, recording or otherwise, without the prior permission of Gibson Publishing

ISBN 978-0-95750-847-7

This is a work of fiction. All the characters and events depicted in this book are fictional and any resemblance to real people or occurrences is entirely co-incidental. Some locations that appear in the story are real enough, and others have been used rather fictitiously.

Gary Tulley asserts the moral right to be identified as the author of this work.

Special thanks to Sheila my wife, for the support and assistance she has given me in making the book possible.

Thanks also to Julie Shilliam for her frank and valuable appraisal of my manuscript prior to publishing.

My deep appreciation also goes to Margaret Austen for her artistic input on the cover design.

Last but not least, thanks to my publisher Gibson Publishing for services rendered.

And thanks to the rest of my immediate family for keeping the faith.

Once Upon a Spook

Crime / Murder mystery featuring .. Mike Eastern PI

by Gary Tulley

Gibson Publishing

Chapter One
A lifetime

'Old habits die hard' or so we are led to believe. This leaves the cynics amongst us to run with the flipside and live with the consequences. One martyr in particular could now be found reviewing his lifelong membership to the cause. Purely out of habit of course, as he paused to gain breath and curse the world at large. The origin of his untimely outburst was aimed at the second flight of steep stairs leading on to his decrepit office, and sometimes dwelling refuge, dependent on client availability.

The unimaginative one bedroom self-contained flat he rented, could be found situated above a 24/7 Italian 'fast food' outlet. The deal Mike Eastern negotiated at the time suited his requirements, and a much relieved landlord's pocket. Suffice to say, that was some eight years ago, and in leg years "A bleedin' lifetime!" as Eastern would say. So, what do we know about this somewhat elusive and self confessed maverick Private Investigator?

In the past, his allergy to wedding cake had subsequently evolved into three divorce proceedings, all on the grounds of irreconcilable differences. The difference in his case being that he was never around to contest otherwise. "It's all down to my line of business your Honour" would be his standard plea. He finally got the message and opted out of normality as we know it, by embarking on a career as a full time PI. This included a CV ranging from missing persons, crime and marital

A lifetime

issues. The latter being a speciality derived from past experience.

In his younger days, Mike Eastern as he was known then, (the derivation being an extracted form of Marcus Enstien from birth), could be found 'trading' leather as a full time professional boxer. Regrettably, an ongoing eye injury eclipsed a successful career, forcing him into retirement after five years. Sticking with the same theme, he undertook the role employed as a doorman or bouncer, graduating to a security guard in a casino.

The lure of self rule with added financial gain, came about sometime later while acting as a PI. It resulted in a decision that would inevitably determine his ultimate future, and his current bank account.

Having just completed a 24/7 surveillance contract with little to show for his pains, his sofa-cum-bed affirmed one aspect he knew he could rely on. Mastering the steep stairs proved to be a grief bonus. Sighing deeply, he inserted the key to the 'office' door. Brimming with expectancy he gently turned it while anticipating a reaction. It was no more than he'd expected, as the key refused to respond.

"Shit!" he exclaimed loudly. "Poxy lock…if I don't get it sorted soon…" Moments later it relented, enabling him to gain entry. It wasn't so much the acrid smell of stale tobacco smoke that caused him to take a sharp intake of breath. Moreover it issued from the competing odour that rose above it, given out from a half eaten pizza languishing in a state of prolonged culture. Wincing, Eastern picked his way through a trail of dated mail and discarded newspapers. Only a lone empty bottle of Scotch stood in his way as he lunged at the handle of a nearby window.

His well meant intentions nosedived as his situation evolved into a battle of two evils as he forcibly opened the window. Peering out, a cloud of chemical infused steam wafted towards him from an adjacent launderette, partially obscuring a railway viaduct which served as an ominous black cloth set in a sea of grey slate roofs and distinctively clay chimney pots. "Could be worse," he growled. "Thank Christ it's not pissing down, this wall has got enough damp in it to grow bleedin' mushrooms!"

Slowly he peeled off his overcoat and slung it over the solitary chair which doubled up as a tie rack. Rubbing his eyes, he headed for a well beaten filing cabinet. If he'd have been blind he couldn't have made his actions appear any easier. His outstretched hand yanked open a specific drawer in a habitual fashion, allowing him to retrieve a half full bottle of Scotch. "God I needed that!" He remarked somewhat inappropriately as his 'poison' connected with the back of his throat. The remarks only got better with every eager gulp he imbibed, finally finishing with "well that's breakfast sorted, it's time I got my head down for a few hours. I'll check the phone later."

The definition of 'later' in his case extended to almost three hours and beyond, when the only hiatus present came from the insistent sound of his phone kicking in. The first time that it rang only became a precursor for the second and third by allowing his dysfunctional brain time to absorb the fact that reality really does exist.

"Damn!" he declared through bleary eyes. "Can't a man have a day off for Christ's sake?" In his case it was never going to happen, or indeed in anybody's language come to that. Once again his face creased as a direct result from the God given daylight that existed, as he vainly attempted to negotiate the phone through blitzed eyes. Not that he would have been aware or given a damn, as his addled brain could now be found on a sponsored walkabout, lying a few miles south of the Watford gap and the same amount of distance north of planet Mars.

At least his reflexes came out in sympathy as he succeeded in grabbing the phone on his third attempt. "I don't know why I bleedin' bother, it's probably some creep looking for money," he assured himself. Reluctantly he picked up the handset and spoke in a vehement manner. "This is Mike Eastern PI, if you know me then bloody hang up…if you don't, then leave a message." Slamming the phone down, he quickly decided that midday was for people who had a problem in telling daylight and night time apart. "Once you're under the blasted duvet, who gives a shit anyway?" became his defining thought on the matter.

Trying to convince himself that his logic held water fell into a lower league. Any perceived notion that a deal with sleep was back on the cards disintegrated as the ominous ring tone from his phone once again refused to give up the ghost. Question: how the hell do you tell someone to piss off when they're on the receiving end, and you don't want to answer it even under a distress warrant? You could always take it off the hook, but that defeats the object of leaving a message. Still it continued to ring. His negative thinking had now run its course. "Whoever is on the end must have my number confused with the poxy Samaritans" he told himself, with just a hint of acrimony.

It was time to throw the towel in and the caller was handed a reprieve. "If you…" verbal desperation cut him short mid sentence. "Please! I'm begging you Mr Eastern, don't hang up on me…just hear me out." The tone of voice, he quickly deduced, was obviously female by origin. Slowly and trance like he lowered the receiver and cupped it with his free hand. Frowning heavily, he strived to concentrate on his immediate thoughts. Knowing what he knew now, it would have taken more than a translator on hand to sway his perception. Less than five minutes ago he was feeling dead and buried, and even in less time reincarnated on the strength of a voice that reaches out from the back of beyond. The kind that grabs you by the throat and leaves you akin to a punch bag that's well past its sell by date. Eastern, by now realised that his attachment to the caller clearly belonged to a woman of substance. But not just any woman, this particular one just happened to be a high ranking Police Officer's wife, and one not unfamiliar to him from his past.

Once again, it was left to the caller to continue where she had left off, and her previous persistence implied that she wasn't going to go away that easily. "Hello, Mr Eastern…that is Mr Eastern isn't it?" Under the circumstances he now felt obliged to go along with the enquiry purely out of curiosity. Strangely enough, in spite of the verbal tension that existed he now felt the situation was in his grasp. Clearing his throat, he responded in a business type manner.

"Speaking, how can I be of assistance?" At this stage it was paramount that he needed to assure himself that the call was indeed kosher. The idea of being familiar with a woman of standing, known in political circles as being one Mrs Conway, would be nothing short of assisted suicide. It swiftly became clear by her laboured breathing, which Eastern readily picked up on, that the nature of her call was anything but a fund raising scheme for a local charity ball.

"I have to ask you Mr Eastern...are you alone at present?" She enquired in a tentative manner. An uneasy silence ensued as Eastern digested her reasoning. Finally, his strained patience keeled over as he diplomatically decided to keep his thoughts to himself...Alone! You stupid bitch! Three broken marriages behind me and a possible bankruptcy looming and you want to know if I'm holding a poxy celebration party...

"Mr Eastern? Are you there?" The tone of her voice now seemingly registered a plaintiff cry for help as opposed to a question - the effect of which brought Eastern back to ground zero.

"You can talk freely Mrs Conway. I can assure you of that." In a split second, Eastern had gone from a semi deranged person to a full confidante the next. But then this was the real Mike Eastern in full flight, and doing what he was best at. "Please carry on, whatever you have got to say remains confidential, you just need to trust me... okay?"

"Oh dear," she replied, with a hint of anxiety. "It's just occurred to me that you've obviously recognised my voice. I'm not very good at this sort of thing am I?" About as close to being good at this as Brighton is close to China, Eastern thought. Fortunately, her honesty got him out of jail by enabling him to establish a working repartee.

"Believe me Mrs Conway, if I can be of any assistance I will, providing of course..."

"I appreciate your concern Mr Eastern" she cut in. "But what we need to discuss in detail is something I'd rather not talk about over the phone. What I can say, is that you come highly recommended, and I propose..." she broke off at this point. "Assuming of course that you consent to a pre arranged meeting."

By now the handset was so hot it was burning Eastern's hand. The present situation had now accelerated from "What the hell?" to "I can't believe what I'm hearing."

"Mr Eastern?"

"Yeah, sorry, that definitely makes sense, where and what have you got in mind?" Not that he was willing to give a damn, but business being business meant that she reflected pound notes, he reminded himself. And God only knows he needed the dough. The case he was presently involved in would only have stood him two months' rent at best. All he had to do was prove that an 18ct wanker of a husband was screwing his sister in law. "Why the hell don't they do it in daylight? The selfish bastards, then we can all sleep at night," he chided.

Brushing that thought aside momentarily, he reflected on his latest proposition. Briefly he had reservations of a sort. The initial call itself stank of bad timing. "Have I inadvertently subjected my confidence into opening a can of worms?" He mused. Almost at once, his doubts evaporated as his would be client then took control of the situation.

"I suggest that you leave everything to me Mr Eastern, it is imperative that I need to observe a sense of security in this matter, should it prevail. I will be back in touch again shortly. Therefore, any future dealings between us will be in the form of a letter. Once again I thank you for your time and patience."

Their apparent conspiratorial conversation then ended on a clinical note as the line suddenly went dead, leaving him to contemplate what might have been. For a short time, Eastern chose to remain pensive as he gathered his addled thoughts, before finally replacing the receiver. "It's all happened too damn quick, think man…I need to think! Damn the bitch, she's caught me flat footed,' he said to himself. It was never going to be the best of epitaphs, for it could have resulted in a lucrative contract in terms of a monetary injection, plus the added bonus, enabling him to resurrect a business that was by now hammering at the door of the local receiver. True to form, he turned to the only recourse that he'd become accustomed to.

Drawing long and hard on his paternal cigarette, he swirled a copious amount of Scotch around in his glass, and then methodically exhaled small consistent circles of smoke through pursed lips. He seemed almost transfixed, as he watched them rise slowly upwards. By now his brain began working overtime, thus allowing him to juggle his thoughts. Finally, a form of common sense took centre stage, as he spoke with deliberation. "That's where I intend going, up! No more shit, no more favours. As from now, Mike Eastern is open for business, but this time with a rearranged slant."

From that moment on, even his 'poison' seemed to taste that much better, his cigarette was something else. Whatever impact Mrs Conway had seemingly made on him, now consumed his body as his head hit the pillow that night. For the first time in months he slept like a dead man...and dead men reputedly, tell no tales.

To contest that theory would have taken a better man than Eastern, in knowing that his brain had been seduced into serving solitary for the past few months. On awakening the following morning, his decisive new image immediately kicked in as he consulted his watch. It took a double take just to assure him that it was showing just after 6am. As he dressed, he could hear the distinctive vibrant buzz of the city coming to life, as it drifted through a partially opened window. The knock on effect that it gave out, in his case became a commodity that you could only obtain from a bottle, as it readily consumed his prescription body. "Today is going to be the first day of my life", he convinced himself, as he exited his flat an hour later.

At the time, it appeared to be an appropriate statement to make, but on reflection had he known any different, it was one that he would have settled for in triplicate. Unfortunately for him, the adage 'weary is the head that wears the crown' would now through unexpected circumstances come to the fore. And in doing so, headline a premeditated situation, now fully intent on blowing his image sideways. As traits come and go, his gut instinct had in the past served him well, and only got better with age. The time had now surfaced for him to call in a favour once again.

Eastern instantly became alerted to the two dubious looking characters emerging from a parked car, some ten metres or so away as he bided his time with intentions of crossing the road. It became clear to him that their body language resonated grief, as the pair headed toward him, possibly bent on a collision course of some description. Initially his attention had been drawn toward the damaged number plate on the vehicle, which was noticeably devoid of any registration. "Right couple of dummies" he remarked inwardly, "They must be driving the bloody car around for a bet."

For a split second, his thoughts were lost in transit owing to the smell of cooking drifting his way, from the 'OVERDONE RASHER' café, opposite to where he was standing.

"D'ye happen to have a light…Eastern?" The sudden realisation that the intimidating request spelt out a personal message swiftly brought him back down to earth, as the taller of the two alien figures confronted him.

A 'please' would have been acceptable but he responded "Piss off" as a jerk reaction. It sounded good in Eastern's head, he thought as his survival instinct checked into overdrive.

On par, his evergreen brain was already issuing its own overall version of events by confirming that the whole scenario, and bearing in mind the aggressors' method of approach, undoubtedly bore the hallmark of a professional organised 'set up'. He just happened to be the fall guy. At this stage, a one on one physical situation with his tormentor, should it have transpired, was the least of his worries should his prowess be called into judgement. What he hadn't considered, was the untimely role of the second assailant, who by now had just put himself in a position to attack from the rear. In retrospect, the situation now culminated in Eastern's downfall as he attempted to remonstrate.

His vain attempt to level the score was rendered useless, as a well directed cosh collided with virgin flesh and bone. The weapon then smashed into the back of his head with sickening force. The impact imploded inside Eastern's skull creating an immediate paralysis, affecting his arms and legs. Millions of tiny lights ran rampant inside his head, glowing in unison before being swept up into a blanket of designer pain and nausea. Mercifully, his suffering ceased as a rush of darkness swept over his body like a Tsunami. He was unconscious long before the pavement beneath him bore the brunt of his useless body.

Later, coming to terms with the unexplained altercation was one thing, attempting to analyse the reason behind it was proving difficult. Having been released from hospital following a check up, Eastern now sought refuge back in his flat, alongside a bottle of Scotch as a mediator. Finding the answer to a thousand and one unanswered questions, the most prominent being "Why me of all people?" was fast becoming a non plus. In return, the liquor that he freely managed to imbibe only reinforced his convictions by rubbishing any doubts he may have held regarding the origin of the attack.

"I'm convinced that there's a link between the Conway woman and the two 'gorillas' who leaned on me. Somebody out there obviously wants me to ease off the case…full stop. Whoever it was that set me up has got a hell of a lot to lose for one reason or another," he told himself, and concluded, "One thing is for certain, they need to know that I am in this for the long haul. Whoever is pulling the shots has got an uninvited date with karma for what happened to me today."

Even solace liquid has got a cut off point, and Eastern had now reached the terminus. On reflection, his day had proved to be eventful if only for all the wrong reasons. All in all, just another day in the life of a maverick PI. In the end, struggling to play catch up with lead lined eyes was never going to win him any medals. Tiredness finally got the better of him, and he resorted to his make shift bed in the knowledge that sleep would be one aspect he wasn't in a position to contest.

Chapter Two
An 'Eastern' promise

Eastern was beginning to feel like the eternal 'cat on a hot tin roof'. The pensive look that shrouded his face could well be mistaken into fast becoming a permanent feature. Once again he studied his desk diary, drumming his fingers on the desk to release his agitation. "Nine days…it's been nine days, and still no blasted contact from Mrs Conway," he reminded himself. By now, he was beginning to think that his self anointed new image was somehow flawed. "Typical poxy money set, they think that they own you on the strength of one bleedin' phone call. Giving it large one minute, and then hanging you out to dry the next. What she needs is a kosher hormone specialist to straighten her out!"

As if by demand, a cynical smile began to take over his face as he continued to stalk his verbal assassination in a different direction. This time, toward her estranged husband. "I can just see you now Mr flaming DCI Conway, I reckon you're getting more grief right now than I am, poor sucker." Any other thoughts on the subject drifted as the sound of an unfamiliar voice coming from downstairs made itself known.

"Mr Eastern, hello…anybody there?"

"Who the hell wants to know?" Eastern fired back, as he opened the door.

"Rapid Courier service Guv." The voice went on, "I need a signature for a package, I take it you are Mr Eastern?"

Smiling to himself, Eastern replied, "For two bleedin' flights of stairs, I'd better be mate." He proceeded to make his way down to join him. Having taken possession of the package, and thirty six stair treads later, he found himself eyeballing the package, now lying on his desk, with interest. "Uhmn, nice to be wanted," he muttered to himself. "Let's hope that whatever it contains is worth the trouble."
In a second, his fragile existence reverted to being gilt-edged as he allowed the contents to spill out onto his desk. The personal letter heading became the first significant clue as to what he could expect to find. "Well I'll be damned" he retorted. "Looks like her ladyship has come up trumps after all and here's me thinking ain't life a bitch!" Having read through the enclosed letter twice, for suitable clarification, it was time for Eastern to sit back and summarise the contents. The message itself, he noted, that held the key to Mrs Conway's proposed contract, was clearly outlined and precise in its wording:
Dear Mr Eastern,

Due to unforeseen circumstances beyond my control, I apologise for the delay in contacting you once again. I am sure that by now, you can appreciate by the measures I hopefully intend to undertake, that this is not a decision I have arrived at without in depth consideration. Namely, my personal well being. Such is the importance of any binding contract we may possibly enter into. Furthermore, the trust I hope to place in you is paramount to any future developments, that I anticipate arising.

I do not wish to digress at this point into the problems surrounding my dilemma, except to say that you come highly recommended. So it goes without saying, I can expect the best of your service at all times. You will find enclosed certain information detailing directions, and a specific time for a joint meeting at a venue of my own choice. Should you wish to pursue this matter, please do not attempt to contact me beforehand. It is imperative that you respect my concern at this point.

Please note that you have ten minutes beyond the specified time enclosed to sanction my proposed meeting. Should you choose to renege, I will presume that you have no desire to continue with my proposal. That being the case, then this letter and its contents, like

myself, shall become null and void. I sincerely hope that this will not be the case, and therefore I look forward to seeing you again in the foreseeable future.
I remain yours in anticipation,

Mrs J Conway (nee Travers)

From the stalls one minute and the upper circle the next, resulted in a lot to take in, even by Mike Eastern's standards. One thing he could be certain of would be his decision to accept Mrs Conway's contract, which to his mind was etched in granite prior to any form of meeting being on the cards. Eastern nodded approvingly, once having reviewed the additional content. The idea of a nominated 'safe house' namely and out of town country club set in rural Sussex, seemed the ideal solution. Providing, of course, that his timing was right.

Once again, he scanned the letter in the event he'd inadvertently missed anything. It soon became clear that something was amiss. It was as if Mrs Conway's consideration to detail attached to her signature was telling him something.

"Travers?" he mused. "The name certainly rings a bell, but why go to the trouble of including it alongside her married title. Unless of course…" He stopped briefly to allow a flicker of recognition to enter his thinking. "Unless of course she has done it for a reason, expecting me to pick up on it?"

Almost immediately a cryptic smile enveloped his face. "Of course! I should have known better, Travers…retired Chief bloody Constable Travers, she has to be his daughter. Talk about a family affair, this case just gets better by the minute." Having established the location of their covert 'meet' it then became a case of tying up the loose ends on any outstanding business commitments. With so much shit flying around his head, and a 48 hour waiting endurance test in front of him, Eastern began to consider the thought that he may well be on a collision course with a runaway rollercoaster.

His past experience alone should have told him the importance of first impressions, as he surveyed inside the minimalist wardrobe. A curtain strung across what was presumably a larder at one time.

On reflection, it turned out to be a bad call. A look of disdain entered the equation, as he took stock of the situation. "There's more blasted shirts on the floor than there are on hangers," he ranted. "It's about time I got my act together, and as for the suits..." Scratching his head, more out of frustration than despair, he convinced himself that the view of the nearby viaduct from his window had more appeal. Basically, his disinherited problem lay with a woman (Mrs Conway) who had inadvertently interrupted his predictable and selfish way of life.

He now realised that the time had come to face facts. With three failed marriages behind him, what knowledge he held about the female gender could be found written on the back of a postage stamp. "I can't afford to mess up, there's too much riding on this deal" he convinced himself. "Besides," he went on, "The woman reeks of class, working with her on board would be tantamount to a passport being thrown in for entry to a world of normality."

In no time at all his extended hiatus became a reality, as Saturday loomed large. With the prospect of a 40 minute drive facing him, timing was off the essence. It was just after 7 o clock that evening when Eastern finally left the bright lights and stress torn atmosphere of his concrete jungle. Leaving Brighton in his wake, he headed for the depths of the countryside, full of conjecture as a would be companion. Half an hour or so later, even the M23 seemed like history as he linked up with a minor road taking him to his destination.

"In a few minutes' time," he diligently reminded himself, "I'll be face to face with Mrs Conway at last. Assuming of course, everything goes to plan."

Glancing around the periphery of the grounds, in which the club restaurant was situation confirmed Eastern's feelings that the latter had done her homework regarding a covert 'meet'. The 'HUNTER'S RETREAT & COUNTRY CLUB' was only a name, but the half a dozen rollers parked amongst a bevy of other designer cars told him different. "I can just imagine the bollocks that goes on inside here on the quiet. I'd love to be a fly on the wall for 24 hours looking on. I reckon I could afford to retire in six months," was his immediate reaction.

An 'Eastern' promise

Having secured his car, he made a beeline for the entrance and entered the foyer. Almost at once, Eastern found himself confronted by a stocky built security guard, intent on making a name for himself.

"I'm sorry sir this is a members' only facility. I will..." A sardonic look came over Eastern's face as he clinically cut him short, the guard wasn't even allowed the benefit of an extended breath before he found himself forced into a verbal altercation as Eastern hit back:

"Relax sunshine, I did what you do now for a living when Crystal Palace was only a goldfish bowl!"

His inquisitor wasn't going to give up that easily.

"I insist that you show me..." Once again his plea for information fell on deaf ears as a third party voice made itself heard.

"It's okay Roberts, I'll deal with this. Is there a problem sir?" The manager enquired. Eastern averted his eyes towards the jobs worth guard before replying:

"Yeah, there could be as it happens, tell this arsehole to get off my case, otherwise I will. For the record, I'm here for an arranged meeting with a certain Mrs Conway, and I wouldn't like to keep the good lady waiting...right?"

"Absolutely sir," the manager replied in a patronising manner. "If you would like to follow me, I have been informed that Mrs Conway has been expecting you, please, step this way." Eastern found himself ushered through into what appeared to be a small, but intimate room, leading off the main bar. The manager attempted to put Eastern at ease. "Please treat the space as your own sir, should you require a drink, feel free to use the hospitality bell. In the meantime, I will inform Mrs Conway that you have arrived." He then made a swift departure.

Eastern nodded approvingly, and grunted a token 'Thank you." He made himself comfortable. All he had to do now would be to sit back and relax. Needless to say, he wasn't given that opportunity.

"Mr Eastern, I presume?" Full of mixed emotions, he glanced around and found himself confronted by a striking red haired woman, in her early forties he guessed. Ready, and dressed to kill, wearing a hugging navy blue two piece outfit, complimented by an expensive looking jewelled necklace. Her long and shapely legs he noted, started life exuding from a pair of designer white stiletto shoes, and terminated somewhere around her sylph like neck.

Momentarily his mind wandered into a world of extreme sexual fantasy. "Suppose I'm looking at this from the wrong angle and she turns out to be some sort of nymphomaniac who gets off on mixing with the likes of me?" His wishful thinking plummeted to zero as the steward made a hurried return. "Your order madam…sir" Eastern lost no time in topping up his glass with the desired water and went for broke:

"So, what would you like to drink to Mrs Conway?" he enquired. She deliberated before replying in a firm and astute manner.

"A successful conclusion will do for a start, wouldn't you say?"

"And then?"

"Now it is your turn Mr Eastern, I suspect you have a few ideas of your own you may like to share?"

"More than you will ever know lady, but I'll keep them to myself." He wistfully muttered under his breath.

"You were saying?"

"Sorry, I was just thinking out loud, although on a serious note, maybe you can explain to me, why you have gone to so much trouble to make this meeting possible?" Her reply, when it came, side stepped into full business mode.

"Basically Mr Eastern, on the assumption that you decide to take the case, any future dealings on a personal level, will have to be on the same footing as this one."

"I'm not about to argue with that," he assured her, and went on. "Keep talking, I'm a good listener." For reasons of her own, she began to toy with her glass. It became obvious to him that her next approach, when it came, would hold the key to 'Pandora's box'. His intuition, fair to say, couldn't be faulted once she had opened up to him.

"You are obviously aware of who I am by now. The fact that you have met my husband in a professional capacity in the past, and I daresay myself made life easy for me to arrive at my decision."

"Which is?"

"For you to represent me of course."

A quizzical look clouded Eastern's face as he analysed her solid reply. It occurred to him that it included reviewing a hidden question that he needed to qualify.

"Right! So let's get your conclusion in perspective. Are you saying in effect that your husband has got no knowledge of your presence here?" Her stoic demeanour didn't falter in reply.

"I'm saying exactly that Mr Eastern. I am forced to keep my social movements close to my chest, any untoward disclosures would undoubtedly provoke dire consequences."

In one sense her reply, albeit a third party threat, now added a reverse effect as to his thinking and, in doing so, left him slightly relieved. I can guess what this conversation is leading up to, he assured himself. All the signs point to one conclusion. Why the hell doesn't the damn woman come right out with it and say, my husband appears to be screwing around, end of story? That way, we can all go home…bloody drama queen. There and then, Eastern decided to jump the verbal queue by levelling with her. "I presume you want Mr Conway placed under surveillance, with the usual dirty washing thrown in? So, how long has the situation been going on for, and how far do you want me to run with it?"

The designer look that appeared on her face told him what she thought of his impromptu suggestions. The realisation on his part (had he been aware) that his hasty assumption had fallen way short and in the process almost landed him in the proverbial shit. Luckily for him, there was a get out clause, and she was quick to remind him of it.

"I just wish it was that easy Mr Eastern. I can forgive you for thinking otherwise knowing that there is a fifteen year gap in age between my husband and myself. However," she stressed, "You can rule out any theories in that direction."

Lost in translation one minute, to dealing with reality the next, left Eastern having to think on his feet. "I see, your problem obviously goes deeper than I suspected," he ventured, and let her continue.

"To be perfectly frank, my life at this moment in time is in one holy mess, and I…" She faltered, leaving her voice to waver momentarily. The opportunity arose and Eastern took full advantage by invading her space.

"Please, take your time. Think carefully and stick to the facts that matter. Oh, and by the way, your drink is getting cold." He quipped.

It was always going to be a throwaway line, but his gesture seemed to have the desired effect. She soon regained her composure by smiling thankfully, before speaking again.

"God! Where do I start?"

"At the beginning seems to be a good enough place for me," Eastern responded encouragingly. His phoney invitation to her drink then came home to roost as she swiftly emptied her glass of gin. Seconds later, after fumbling around in her handbag, she eventually produced an envelope, and handed it to him.

"Here, I would like you to read the contents, and then we can discuss your views. What I can tell you now, is that it hasn't been sent to me by someone who is interested in my welfare. On the contrary." It wasn't going to be the first of its type that Eastern had encountered. In his experience, he deduced that the content needed to be taken seriously from the offset. Gorging on apprehension, Mrs Conway looked on as Eastern proceeded to read the letter.

Mrs Conway, I strongly advise you to treat this letter seriously. Should you not choose to do so, the implications you will lay on yourself including your family will come into play. And, at worst, life threatening. I stress, this affair is not about money Mrs Conway. For my part, I am terminally ill, and therefore have no regrets in not seeking financial gain from you. More importantly than that, I am seeking a form of retribution on behalf of my late father, who through circumstances instigated by your despicable husband (and others) induced him into taking his own life. Believe me, when I say this, but I intend taking extreme measures to ensure the guilt my father carried having been 'fitted up' for a crime he didn't commit, to be over turned. Then, his innocence made public, by every possible means open to me. Including an 'eye for an eye' scenario. The only remaining option available to you, in bringing about a satisfactory conclusion to this matter, would entail a written and witnessed confession by your husband, in clearing my father's name. I sincerely hope that common sense will prevail. As I stated previously, I have nothing to lose or indeed need to justify any action I see fit to take. The decision is yours alone. The instructions that you need, when replying to this letter as to your actions are enclosed. Any outside interest, namely the police or others will only bring my stated intentions forward, when seeking justice....Yours, WINNER.

Eastern's face remained grim looking for a short while, allowing him to screen his thoughts. It was blatantly clear by his body language that the document had left its mark. The disclosure attributed to the police, and even more so Mrs Conway's estranged husband, had now dented his own beliefs in their past relationship. The claim, he considered, had now become a personal issue. Mrs Conway meanwhile was showing a degree of impatience, and eagerness for Eastern to reveal his thoughts.

"So, tell me, what is your immediate reaction?"

He pondered briefly for a few seconds before stating his case. "I'd be a liar if I'd said that I hadn't read better. On a more serious note, it's certainly unique that money isn't a prime factor, although his dedication for retribution bothers me considerably. I think we are looking at a highly volatile individual. It is evident to me that he is somebody not to be messed with."

Sighing deeply, she nodded in accordance. "I suppose..." stopping short, she offered up her 'get out of jail card'. "Is there any way his demands could be a hoax?" Her plea became a card too far, as Eastern explained in no uncertain terms.

"Nice to think so, but no. Whoever wrote this, to my mind, is well educated, and obviously has done their homework. Which puts you in a messy position regarding your husband. Incidentally, why didn't you hand the letter over to him in the first place?"

She stalled for time, it was almost as if Eastern had hit a raw nerve. Her answer, when it came, duly manifested more untold grief. "I couldn't, for selfish reasons alone, my position became untenable in knowing that Mr X's claim ties in with certain knowledge I'm aware of, regarding my husband allegedly 'fitting up' his father."

"Evidence you say! In what way?" Eastern remonstrated. "If you know something that I should know about, you'd better tell me."

"Would you mind if I have another drink first? I'm finding this aspect rather stressful," she pleaded. Having regained her composure, she carried on where she had left off. "You have to understand Mr Eastern, that I was young and so naïve when I first married. But as time progressed, I realised that nobody goes from being a 'bobby' on the beat to the rank of a DCI in the time it took my husband to achieve. And then of course, there's his father to consider as well."

"Him! Being the assistant Chief Constable as well." At this point, Eastern's mind was still at full stretch, he knew deep down, exactly what she was implying without her justifying it. And the idea of a 'bent' cop or two, could become a reality, by giving more credence to the basis of this letter. "Our Mister X, for want of a name, hasn't exactly made life easy for you, or indeed myself should I take the case. I mean, whatever happened to good old fashioned blackmail? This case has got more facets than a cut diamond. I can fully understand why you distanced yourself from your husband. If at any time there was something untoward going on in the ranks, and Mister X is adamant there was, then the likelihood of any fresh evidence arising would be trashed."

He paused long enough to throw his Scotch back, and looked at her long and hard. "I think I need another drink, this is beginning to sound like a very bad nightmare." His fresh Scotch, only served to dampen his throat, leaving his personal headache to increase, as he tried to make sense of the bare facts. 'Joe Public' was one thing when it came to business, but the added grief of police intervention at the same time could lead to consequences of a personal and disturbing nature. "In theory," he told himself, "It would be like trying to walk an electrified tightrope with no off switch. And I ain't no bloody circus act."

Mrs Conway then thankfully brought him down to earth. "It's not looking good is it? I can clearly see that you are having reservations about taking the case."

Eastern then made an effort to put her mind at rest. "If I consent, I will of course require a private contact number, and a joint arrangement on any decisions that arise. In the meantime, I will put a few feelers of my own out. Depending on my findings, I will contact you in 48 hours, and give you a concrete decision one way or another. As far as your domestic scene goes, just act natural, but keep a low profile if socialising."

Driving back home that night, Eastern's journey seemed to fly by.

His evening overall had been an eye opener in more ways than one, starting from the moment Mrs Conway had introduced herself. "A working man's sexual fantasy, classy with it, but somebody I could place my trust in," summed up his reference.

Right now though, he had his sights set on far more important issues. With only two days remaining to come up with some answers to induce a decision of a lifetime would mean intense delving into the unknown on his part. "Have I got the bollocks to see it through?" became his opening gambit, as he recalled the previous incident to warn him off the case. "One thing I can be sure of, this case is either going to make or break me." He concluded, "Oh, what the hell! What have I got to lose anyway?"

This was an ironic statement to arrive at, should one consider the possibility that the one person he would be compensated for in bringing down is exploiting the same line. For a betting man, that could prove to be one double you wouldn't want to put your money on. Imagine this if you will: two individuals each sharing the same verbal persona, except to say, that one is legal (generally) and the other is a would-be felon. There has to be a winner, but therein lies the problem...so, which one would you personally back, having surveyed the facts?

Chapter Three
Two meetings and one mind

Without question Eastern was feeling the heat. The morning following the 'meet' was deemed to be the first day of the rest of his life. As from now, Eastern would be on a non-negotiable deal with the devil 24/7. With 24 allotted hours remaining in which to obtain a kosher lead of any kind, things were not looking good. A spoonful of broken promises via an alcoholic 'snout' wasn't exactly a passport to success. The only positive in return, was that his room appeared to have more appeal, as he surveyed his desktop through bleary eyes.

A collage of plastic coffee cups, some still half full, complimented an array of discarded dog ends, that had once found life in the various empty cigarette packets, now seeking refuge amongst a multitude of scrap note paper. The layered pall of smoke that hung between the floor and the ceiling, became an extra by giving a new dimension to his office. Purely by luck, his eyes fell on a tatty calling card, lying half hidden amongst the debris. It seemed to hold a form of fascination within its content, as he reached out to retrieve it. Turning the card over, the contact number he espied had the same effect on his body, by leaving an adrenalin rush.

"Shit! How the hell did I miss that? Bloody Detective Sergeant (DS) Johnnie Curtis, now there's a guy who owes me from way back. Yeah, about time I called in a favour." Patience was running at a premium as the phone continued to ring. "Pick the damn thing up can't you…oh, sorry, Mike Eastern speaking."

"Mike? Mike...yeah, I'm with you now. Christ! It's been a few months mate, what's occurring? I presume you're still in business?"

"Just about, (at least he was honest). You know how it is, same shit different day. Right now, I need to call in a favour Johnnie, I'm desperate. The case I'm involved with at the moment could prove to be my pension, know what I mean?"

"I don't have a problem with that Mike, I still owe you from the 'Lansbury' Bank job. Just how big a favour are you looking for anyway?"

"Big wouldn't even be close mate. Quite frankly, I'm seeking some information contained in a specific file."

"Bloody hell Mike! You laid that one on me, you do realise that I'm based at HQ now? Blimey mate, you've got more chance of winning the National, riding a blasted donkey! I'm sorry mate, but that's more than my job is worth...you know that."

Eastern wasn't going to give up that easily, by deciding to push their friendship. "I hear what you say, but I'm asking for all the right reasons. We both know that you have 'friends' downstairs, and that's the only reason I'm asking. Believe me, it's imperative that I secure the information I'm looking for." His perseverance at this juncture appeared to pay off as Curtis appeared a trifle sympathetic.

"It's obvious we are not talking about a two up and two down domestic here," he supposed. "I get the distinct impression that you're into something 'heavy', from what I can gather." At this stage, Eastern decided to keep tight lipped about his suspicions, unless challenged and allowed Curtis to continue. "I make no promises Mike, I'll do what I can, but you know the rules. If this deal winds up in the karzy, you're on your own...understand? In fact, we never had this conversation full stop. Now, you'd better give me some details before I change my bloody mind."

Eastern then went on to state the SP (information) he was seeking revolved around a certain prime suspect, who was found guilty of murder, made possible by damning evidence put forward by the Crown. The fact that the accused subsequently committed suicide a few months after being sent down, held the key to the file in question.

He also went on to say that a certain DSI Conway was a key figure in handling the case. More importantly, the name of the alleged guilty party was paramount.

Jotting a few relayed notes down was the easy part, DS Curtis then once again laid Eastern's request on the line. "This could take some time Mike. The fact that you haven't mentioned when the case itself initially opened could prove to be a stumbling block. Just for the record, and merely an observation you understand, the name Conway suggests the word grief in itself. I feel sure that I had a run in with the guy some years ago. As I recall, he was an ambitious bastard at the time anyway, leave it with me, I'll be in touch." He then hung up.

Their conversation had proved invaluable, and more than he could have hoped for. Suddenly, Eastern was beginning to feel like the 'cat that got the cream.'

"If anybody can get a result then Johnnie Curtis is the man in the frame. The sooner he can get some SP back to me the better," was prominent in his mind. In spite of being handed a progressive boost, he was under no illusion as to the undertaking facing him. With that in mind and the prospect of a fruitful phone call in the offing made short work of the weekend and then it all too soon became Monday.

The desired telephone number had become a fixation in his mind, but that didn't stop his hand from visibly shaking as he dialled the required digits.

"Mrs Conway speaking, how can I help?" Ignorant as to the origin of the landline, he'd already decided to let the recipient open the account up until he knew otherwise.

"Hi, it's Mike Eastern here…is it okay to talk?"

"Oh, hello there." She seemed a trifle surprised after he'd made himself known and continued. "I'm sorry, you kind of caught me on the hop. I really didn't expect you to get back in touch…but yes, feel free to speak." In return, it wasn't the best reception he could have asked for and it showed in his thoughts. What the hell was wrong with the damn woman?

"Are you still there?" she interjected.

"I think we've both got off to a bad start Mrs Conway, I thought

I made it quite clear that I would give an answer irrespective of my decision."

"And I apologise for knowing that you stated just that, I can only hope the decision you have reached is a favourable one."

"Well, just to put your mind at rest, after carrying out some research, and the financial side of things are agreeable, I'd be willing to take your case on board with a couple of provisos thrown in as well."

"That's more than I could hope for Mr Eastern…when could you possibly make a start?"

"As far as I'm concerned Mrs Conway, I already have, and rest assured that wheels are turning as we speak."

"In that case, I suggest we arrange another meeting as soon as possible. Since we last spoke a financial development has surfaced. I don't wish to pursue the facts over the telephone, but only to say that its relevance is vital to the case. I'll get back to you tonight, say about 8.30pm with some instructions to see you the following night. Thank you again Mr Eastern, you'll find that I am a very appreciative woman."

Whether he took the single reference the wrong way or not, he did at least have the last word on the matter as he hung up. "Yeah and I've only been divorced three times your Ladyship, this is one relationship that'll be strictly business!"

At the eleventh hour, Eastern made a rapid decision to ditch his car in favour of a cab for convenience sake. "I've got more chance of finding God than getting a parking space in Brighton!" he thought sardonically. The prearranged meeting set up by Mrs Conway, was a small Bistro type restaurant, set in the heart of the Kemptown area to the east of the City, and well known for its gay provenance.

Eastern gave himself one last look in the mirror, and grimaced as a two way battle of dress code looked like taking a hammering. The eventual winner became an off-white suit backed up by a yellow open necked shirt. "I don't believe I'm bloody doing this," he growled. "I'll put this lot down to expenses. She's got me believing I'm the oldest 'queen' in town, what a way to make a poxy living!"

15 or so minutes later, and he was paying the cab off. The restaurant

itself was situated at the end of a cul-de-sac, and apart from a dismal lantern hanging forlornly above the main door, the venue itself melted into the shadows of the adjacent buildings. "I've got to hand it to her she's done her homework again, you wouldn't find this 'gaff' in broad daylight, let alone bleedin' night time." With mixed emotions he entered the bistro and booked in under a chosen pseudonym. He'd almost finished his first drink when she finally made an appearance.

Any formal debate became lost on a 'double take' as Mrs Conway apologised for her delay. Eastern was briefly struggling for words, as a wave of expensive perfume filled his nostrils, while the outfit that she was 'nearly' wearing was something else.

"That's fine...forget it, and by the way the wait was worth it." Moments later the reference came back to bite him in the arse as he recalled his previous singular approach to their contact namely, "Never mind the gloss, just think pound notes." Easy to say when said quickly, and he would be the first to admit that for a lady, she's one hell of a chick, and all woman at that.

Needless to say, the following few hours slotted into good food and drink, while enjoying pleasant banter with the wine doing a better job than a prompt. "You looked as if you enjoyed that Mike." She then checked herself, "I'm sorry that was forward of me, I..." Mike didn't flinch.

"I wouldn't dwell on it, you'll only spoil a quality evening besides which, that is what my closest friends call me...tell you what, here's the deal. I'm Mike and..."

"You can call me Joan if you like," she offered in return. They then both shook hands. He wished somehow that she wouldn't let go.

"I'll settle for that, yeah I like that...Joan. Now then, business! You mentioned on the phone that you've got some fresh information for me?" He laughed, "let's hope it's as good as our last deal." Mrs Conway nodded and smiled in agreement before speaking.

"Basically, it concerns my estranged husband's financial affairs."

"Right! So there is a strong connection between that, and the case as a whole?"

She was doing her best to remain convincing. "Indirectly I'm compelled to say yes, I get the feeling he's involved in a money making scheme, and has been for some time," she stressed.

"A backhander fever comes to mind." He mused. "Have you any proof, and if you have, how does it tie him in with this case?"

"I'll let you be the judge of that Mike, I came across a strange phone number purely by chance, inside the drawer of a bureau I happened to be clearing out. It had obviously been there for some time. Intrigued as I was, I then dialled the number."

"And?" Eastern was like a dog on a leash at this stage.

"Would you believe it belonged to a Swiss bank?"

Eastern woefully shook his head, "He certainly had you fooled Joan, but my instincts are telling me that your husband is verging on being 'bent' as we say, but why I ask myself. I honestly think that this whole scenario is all about getting illegitimate results, capped off by a fast track promotion from the same source. I'd give anything to know how many innocent people he's managed to put away."

"Well, even though we don't know the name of Mister X yet, we do at least know of one person he's managed to 'fit up' as you might say."

Eastern offered up a wry smile before responding. "You've been busy reading too many Detective books Joan, but you are right of course. As for the missing name, that dilemma has been haunting me as well. Fortunately, I'm expecting a call at any time, so we can hopefully lay that one to rest. Plus of course, a respectable lead."

"That appears to be interesting, but what do you intend doing in the meantime?"

He leaned forward as if to make a point. The tone of his voice then took on a serious note as he replied. "Worry about your health for one thing, all the time that maniac I'm looking for has got breath, he's acting like a thinking man's copper, and pulling all the strings at the same time."

"Just supposing I..." she faltered midway.

"Yeah, carry on, it can't be that bad."

"What if I come clean and show my husband the letter? At some stage, I'm going to have to surely." Eastern was adamant as he expressed his feelings.

"Absolutely no way! Certainly not yet anyway. As for the offshore account you can save that one to the last. The way I figure it, this maniac needs to keep you in one piece as his go between. You are his only way through to the core of this whole problem, which is central to your husband. The less he's aware of what is going on in the background the better. Time is of the essence in your case and I need a name, like, yesterday. Once I've established that, then the 'mind games' begin to surface."

"Mind games? You've lost me Mike."

"I'll explain that another time, in the meantime, we need to set up a convenient chat line, it's imperative that you connect with him. The minute that Mister X feels isolated, is the time when the curtain comes down…end of."

"You make it all sound so easy Mike," she replied admiringly.

Shaking his head, he then beckoned to a nearby waiter, "I don't know about you Joan, but I fancy a nightcap. And to get back to your observation, the secret is never underestimate who you're dealing with."

"I hope I'm included in that," she exclaimed sheepishly, and together they laughed.

"There was one other detail that's just occurred to me. Do you have a close friend, someone you can trust explicitly who is willing to put you up for a couple of weeks, or failing that, your own side of the family maybe?"

"That wouldn't be a problem, I happen to have a journalist friend who's based in Bloomsbury. She also retains a flat in Hove she uses as a bolthole. I'm sure she wouldn't mind me using it." Eastern heaved a sigh of relief and continued.

"That sounds ideal, I must say I feel a lot happier in knowing that. The less your husband knows who, and what you're involved with, the better I like it."

"Problem! It's just occurred to me…mail! If Mr X gets back to me while I'm away what then?"

"That's a chance you're going to have to take, the aim is to contact him. Once we've done that I can open up a post box number, so any further mail is directed to me. I guess that covers everything Joan, but bell me tomorrow without fail so I know that you're organised your end, okay?"

Ten minutes later, having said their goodbyes, he left her in the comfort of a cab. For his part, Eastern decided to walk the meal off, by heading towards the seafront and Grand Parade.

The night air seemed to give his body a lift as he strode along, he felt good about himself, and felt conveniently relaxed for the first time in months. In spite of the many unanswered questions, and conclusions swirling around in his head, he managed to sleep like a baby that night. Even the stairs leading up to his flat seemed that much shorter. As for the door lock, that still managed to retain a mind of its own.

Chapter Four
A break through

Utter frustration, or just severely pissed off? With no options available to him, Mike Eastern was feeling totally inadequate. Almost a week had lapsed, following his covert request for information, surrounding a certain closed file. No news is good news, would be the reply to every optimist with time on their hands. The theory was never going to wash with Eastern. Living and surviving as he did on a day to day basis, with no set rules thrown in. On a positive note, Joan Conway's part time security arrangements had now become a reality. On advice, she had managed to install herself in a 'safe house', albeit a friend's flat in Hove. Her husband meanwhile, was left to his own alleged designs, to ponder on the outcome arising from a marriage of convenience.

Mike Eastern replaced the receiver, having had a lengthy conversation with Joan. A smug look creased his face, "At least she will be safer there for the time being, and the bonus of some breathing space. The poor bitch has inherited the mother of all poxy headaches." He convinced himself.

Minutes later, his phone kicked off leaving him stranded in thought. "I reckon she's probably forgotten to tell me something," became his initial reaction. In anticipation, he lunged at the receiver, "Joan?" A pregnant pause then followed.

"Hello…I seem to have dialled the wrong number," came the reply. The tone of the voice was instantly recognisable by Eastern, as being that of DS Curtis no less.

"No!...no wait mate." Eastern responded and continued "It's me, Mike! I thought you were someone else. As it happens, you couldn't have phoned at a better time Johnnie. Please God you've got some information for me?"

"Yeah I gathered that would be your reaction. But what's with the Joan?"

"Uhm...strictly business...a client," came back an unconvincing reply.

"Oh I see, and I'm bloody Hercule Poirot am I? You said that about your first three wives as I recall." Any reference to his marital track record went clean over his head, as Eastern continued to press for a result.

"Get real mate, listen, did you manage to obtain the SP I requested?"

"Yeah eventually, and not before calling in a few favours of my own. That's why it's taken so long to get back to you."

"You don't surprise me, it was never going to be a walk in the park. At best, I should imagine it was an education in patience...right?"

"As it happens, yeah, but I could have done without the grief... know what I mean? It almost..."

"I'm beginning to," Eastern interjected. "Sorry, carry on mate."

"Well, it turns out your hunch was kosher Mike, knowing what's transpired. It turns out that DCI Conway, has been making a name for himself over the years, in more ways than one. Even accounting for a brief observation, and your case in particular, we're talking missing statements, plus misuse of forensic evidence. And I'm only scratching the surface thus far. It's almost as if Conway has been given carte blanche to an open cheque book."

"I always knew there was more to the guy than a bleedin' peaked hat."

"Yeah right, but the point I'm making from where you're standing, will be one of self preservation, if you intend on pursuing the case. You know the score better than anyone Mike, you're on the outside looking in, remember. Basically, like it or not, the moment they sniff out grief on their doorstep, they're bound to close ranks."

"You said they! So we're talking involvement here then?"

"Absolutely no question about it, there's no way that your man Conway is a solo act. I'm adamant, that this is a cover up on a major scale. Personally, I reckon the system is flawed from the top downwards. I hope for your sake it doesn't turn out to be messy...me? I'd rather walk away."

Before their candid conversation came to a close, Eastern, oblivious to third party reasoning, had no intention of being swayed. Maybe the engaging presence of Joan had some bearing on his decision...who knows? In the event, he was always going to have the last word on the matter in justifying his maverick persona. "Bring it on, to hell with the grief!"

Pouring the tried and tested Scotch into his glass was the easy bit. It only got harder when he finally realised that the said bottle became empty. Unlike his head, which contained more residual shit than his brain was allowed at any one time.

The all important disclosure made possible by Curtis now seemed light years away, including other numerous internal problems. He also reflected on the possible inclusion of a public health warning, should he through dogged persistence recreate a mire of conspiracy, morphing into a lake of corruption.

Depending on one's values, there was always going to be a price to pay, and in this case, the 'piper' was in a position to call the tune!

"They have got away with who they are! By what they are!" Eastern declared vehemently, they being the alleged conspirators. "To my mind that was their first mistake. At least I know now who I'm dealing with. Their second mistake is not knowing that I'm in the opposite corner. My problem lies with how I handle the approach, without causing over exposure. I could use a 'face', a person working on the inside, somebody I could trust...question is, who?"

His bloodshot eyes remained neutral, as once again he scanned the facts of the case, as supplied by Curtis. More so, in a measure of sympathy towards the prime victim, him being the deceased father of the elusive and demanding Mister X. Although the victim's suicide was a fairly recent occurrence, the origin of his case in question extended back to almost six years' prior.

Classified by the police as being an opportunist burglar, at the time of his arrest, Henry Dowling, as he is now identified, was subsequently charged and tried at the Old Bailey, for the wilful murder of one Jacob Spelling, known to be trading as an underworld diamond dealer, up until his untimely death. As a result, and due to a fast track trial, Dowling was unanimously found guilty, and received a statutory life sentence.

The prosecution had claimed that the latter was in the vicinity of the ground floor flat rented by Spelling, on the night of the murder. On the grounds of Dowling's testimony, this claim, when put forwards (for reasons unknown) was never in dispute by his own defence. The transcript went on to say that, while acting on an anonymous tip off, the police apprehended the accused inside the flat in question, whereupon he was duly arrested after discovering Spelling's dead body. A further inspection at the crime scene discovered a damaged window to the rear of the building and was judged to be the means of entry.

On the strength of a post mortem, the pathologist report indicated that the victim had died from a single stab wound to the back of the body, deriving from a Stiletto type paper knife. The time of death itself was proved to be consistent with Dowling's alleged forced entry and the arrival of the police on the scene. Strangely enough, Dowling's defence council then did a 180 degree turnaround by dismissing the pathologist report as rubbish and went on to highlight the latter's original statement to the police:

When I arrived at the rear of the flat, I came across a knife lying in the grass below a window which I found to be wide open. There was broken glass lying around outside as well which I thought was weird, making me think it had been forced open from the inside. Normally, I'm strictly a front and back door man but seeing as the window was open I decided to take advantage of it. Why I pocketed the knife I can't say really, maybe I thought it might have been of some value. Anyway, having got this far I decided to turn the joint over, in spite of the fact that somebody had obviously already beaten me to it. As far as the murder weapon was concerned, I took it to be part of the spoils and had been dropped by whoever broke in before me. Once I got inside I started to get busy but soon realised I was wasting my time. The 'gaff' (flat) had been well trashed and was in a shit state. I found the body of whom I presumed to be the owner, some five minutes later. Even in the bad light I sensed he was 'brown bread' (dead). The geezer's body looked to be propped up in a high backed chair. It didn't look natural like, almost as if somebody had placed him there, know what I mean? Saying that, I couldn't have known that he was brown bread, I'd only been guessing. It was only when the 'bill' (police) showed up and investigated, then I was told the poor bastard was mullered with a knife. So help me guv, I never laid a finger on the guy, physical ain't my style, you know that from my previous… end of statement.

As was the case, Dowling's 'not guilty' plea was rejected after the jury agreed to the prosecution's summing up. That in the accused case it was simply an attempted burglary that had gone disastrously wrong. In addition, the police had discounted the claim of a third party involvement. In spite of forensics showing that besides the victims, and Dowling's being prominent, a third fingerprint was also highlighted on the handle of the murder weapon. Because of its poor clarity, (as suggested by the police) at the time. They stated that they were reluctant to pursue that line of enquiry, for reasons alluding to unsafe evidence.

Sheer frustration, coupled with acute anger, was at a premium, as Eastern digested the alleged facts. And he wasn't about to hold back. "Trial! That was no fucking trial, it was a pathetic showcase of convenience…it stinks of corruption! The police literally crucified Dowling, from the moment he was arrested. As for his mentality at the time, that alone justified a poxy hearing. No sane felon would enter a building on the assumption that 'someone had beaten me to it'. That's total bollocks! It's obvious the man wasn't capable of murder, then, or at any other time in his career. His biggest mistake, if at all, was to admit his intentions."

"And then of course there's the broken window scenario to consider. I see that there's no evidence to support the claim that Dowling had forced it open. (This theory was put forward by the prosecution). I think that Dowling got it right, and that the window itself had been staged to look as if he had indeed forced it open."

"To my mind, a visual lack of proof gives credence to a third party, as being a suspect. And of course, being the murderer, while at the same time depositing the knife as a plant to substantiate his motive. That being the case, then the victim Spelling would more than likely have known his killer."

Eastern paused briefly to gather his thoughts, reaching out he withdrew a prescription cigarette from a nearby jacket, and robotically lit up. Drawing long and hard, he allowed the smoke to fully coerce his lungs, allowing his beleaguered brain to hone in another possible aspect before exhaling.

"Of course!" he exclaimed, in a matter of fact manner. "How the hell did I let that one slip by me?" The reference that had prematurely alluded him, was in tune with the statement made by the police, regarding their approach to the partial fingerprint allegedly found on the murder weapons. "As conclusions go, we have only go their word on that." He pondered in thought. "What if that theory could be proved to be believable and forensic proved that the 'dab' belonged to a known individual?"

Not only could that person be in the frame as the prime suspect. But it also implied he'd be left wide open, into becoming eligible, for flaming membership to the DCI Conway club! "It all makes sense to me now, if ever a guy was 'fitted up' bears out my theory, that Dowling was in the wrong place at the wrong time. The real murderer must have just left via the front door when he heard Dowling entering by the window. I bet the lucky bastard couldn't believe his luck. I guarantee that call he made minutes later resulted in him having a gilt-edged alibi, thrown in for nothing."

The following morning Mike Eastern was engaged in another lengthy conversation, having contacted Curtis regarding his take on the alleged evidence. "So you can well understand my problem Johnnie. It's now become two fold on the one hand, I've got a bent cop that badly needs straightening out, and on the other a terminal maniac who's going to stop at nothing in seeking a result for his late father. It's fast becoming a poxy nightmare in knowing who to play first."

In reply, Curtis, although sympathetic, was also blunt. "I didn't want to be the one to say 'I told you so' Mike. It was always going to be a Catch 22 scenario. I'm afraid you should have seen it coming mate, but for what it's worth, plus the fact that you know who you're dealing with at last. My hunch tells me that your Mr X is the man with all the answers."

"That's a good call Johnnie, I had a feeling you were going to say that." Eastern agreed.

"You know it makes sense Mike, by concentrating on nailing the sick bastard, like it or not, the police would need to get involved at some stage…"

"…And in doing so, leave Conway and his sidekicks in a vulnerable position." Eastern interjected.

"Precisely! Providing of course, Conway doesn't smell a rat, in which case who's to say he's not desperate enough, to eliminate our Mister X?"

"Shit! That's one hell of a serious consideration mate, but yeah, I wouldn't rule it out."

"Well there you go," Curtis emphasised. "Because when you think about what he's got to lose if his little game goes belly up, you know as well as me that controlled 'accidents' usually follow. Oh, there is one other thing I need to mention."

"Namely?"

"You! By that I mean you personally Mike."

"Sorry mate, you've lost me." Curtis then came across as being solicitous in his approach. "Put it this way, you know my feelings on this unholy mess. I figure that one bent cop is as bad as it gets. And knowing your maverick persona, you can't afford to fuck it up. Because all of a sudden, you could become a lousy statistic."

"Thanks for the vote of confidence mate, but your bang in order as usual, anyway it's…" he tailed off in knowing he was about to open a can of worms.

"No, go on," Curtis insisted. "Finish what you started."

"I was only going to say that it's not all about me, there's my client to consider as well." There's no fool like an old fool and Curtis was immediately on his case.

"Where is this leading to Mike? Why do I get the feeling that I've heard this speech so many times before? You're way out of your league mate…business is one thing, and women…"

"Are fucking expensive, I hear you, but I worry about her. You know how it is?" Curtis wasn't convinced and decided that Eastern was in a better position to argue his case.

"On your head be it my son, and if you're looking for a best man, then I come cheap," he jokingly replied.

They continued to talk shop for a while, and unanimously agreed that mutual contact was the best policy. Their conversation was curtailed. The impact arising from his decision to carry the case forward had now come home to roost. Maybe it was deemed that it would take the likes of an outsider such as Curtis to mark his card for him. If only merely as a gesture of exported confidence. The reality is, he was now on his own with everything to prove.

A cryptic smile crossed his face, and he grunted in exasperation as he released his thoughts once more. "What the ruddy hell have I let myself in for?" he questioned himself. Half an hour later, his would-be problems seemed to have disintegrated as the benefit deriving from a liquid lunch chose to leave its personal mark.

Chapter Five
A lead in the right direction

Not that Eastern expected him to be there anyway, living or otherwise. As circumstance unfolded, his assumption became a lesson in elimination. In return a feeling of association with the elusive Mr X, nee Dowling. "A property can tell you an awful lot about its owner. Horses for courses" as you might say. "It's all there. Personality, standards...you name it."

Having obtained Dowling's last known address via the local electoral roll (in this case three years earlier, it matched up with his late father's, given at the time of his arrest). Eastern's pursuit, now entailed a grass roots investigation, as a datum point. Two weeks had now lapsed since Joan had received the initial contact letter, threatening herself and her immediate family. If her estranged husband had held relevant information relative to the case, then he was keeping it close to his chest in her absence.

"At least it keeps you out of the limelight for the time being," Eastern would remind her later, when in conversation. The all important address that he'd been trying to locate turned out to be a mid-terraced Victorian dwelling. Set on three floors, and leading off the Seven Dials area, adjacent to the rear of the Brighton main line station. From the sparse SP that he'd managed to glean, the records showed the residence in question (like the majority in the locale) could be found to be sub-divided into flats.

Eastern winced, and cursed under his breath. With six door bells to choose from, and no tenant title to aid him, left him giving way to utter frustration. "Just my poxy luck! Ah well, in it to win it." Ramming his digit home on the bell of flat two, he twiddled his thumbs while waiting for a response, if any. Patience, as they say, is a virtue. In his case, and some five minutes later, found him rewriting the script. "Huh, that was a bleedin' waste of time." And he turned on his heel to leave.

As he did so, an alien voice drifted up from the basement area below, causing him to stop in his tracks. "Looking for anyone in particular?" the stranger enquired.

Eastern popped his head over the safety rail, and glanced down. He noted that the voice belonged to a scruffy middle aged individual, intent on sweeping the walkway.

"Yeah, I am as it happens," Eastern replied cautiously. "Maybe you can help me?"

A quizzical look appeared on his face as the stranger fired back, "Are you the bloody police?"

Shaking his head resolutely, Eastern attempted to put the man at ease. "God no! But it seems that the person I'm trying to contact is obviously not in."

"What did you say his name was?"

"I didn't, although I was led to believe that a certain Mr Dowling rented flat two." Crossing his fingers, he hoped that his bluff had paid of. Almost immediately the man's eyes lit up.

"Huh! You're wasting your time there guv, he pissed off over a month ago, and the flat's been vacant ever since. I don't suppose you'd know if he was still in the vicinity would you?"

"Why do you say that?"

"Well it was common knowledge that the geezer was living on borrowed time, poor bleeder had the big C I think. Mind you, he never really got over the way that his old man died. Nasty old business that, it's not every day that you get 'banged up' for life. No wonder he topped himself."

"Well that bears out the facts in Dowling's letter to Joan," Eastern said to himself. And ignited his desire to continue their conversation.

"Really? Suicide eh? I don't suppose you would have a forwarding address to hand?" The stranger chuckled and shook his head, leaving Eastern to surmise that he was on a hiding to nothing.

"Is the Pope Jewish? No chance mate, here one minute, gone the next...know what I mean? Tell you what, you might want to try the pub on the corner for what it's worth. That's about as far as he usually went. Weird sort of bloke as I recall, what I call a mystery, know what I mean? You'd never get to the bottom of him."

Eastern had heard enough by now and acknowledged the stranger's assistance. "Thanks anyway, as you say, it's worth a try...bye now." Not feeling too overly disappointed, he turned on his heel and set off in the direction of the pub.

A couple of minutes later found a disenchanted Eastern seeking his first compulsive drink that morning.

"Yes sir, what's it going to be?" the landlord enquired.

"Scotch and dry please, and hopefully you can mark my card at the same time. I'm trying to trace a regular punter of yours. He goes by the name of Dowling." Eastern replied, in a somewhat patronising manner. Then continued in the same vein "Rumour has it, he's moved on recently."

"Yeah I can vouch for that," the landlord readily sanctioned. "He certainly hasn't been using the pub for the last two weeks, not that I'm grieved you understand."

"Hum, that's very interesting, why do you say that?" Eastern ventured.

"Truth is, he was getting to be a bloody nuisance...upsetting the regulars...mouthing off, that sort of thing. It's just as well he's gone, he wouldn't have reigned here much longer. It was obvious that the guy had issues of some kind."

"That bad eh, even more reason why I..."

"Tell you what," the landlord intervened before Eastern could finish, and indicated a nearby table which was taken up by a voluptuous looking blonde. "For what it's worth, it might pay you to have a word with the lovely Rita. She just happens to be on everyone's case, if you know what I mean?"

"Yeah, I get your drift and thanks, I might just do that." Picking up

A lead in the right direction

his Scotch from the bar, a cynical Eastern made his way across. "Rita, isn't it?" he enquired delicately.

"Only to people who know me," came back the curt reply. In anticipation, Eastern placed a £20 note between her 'open plan' heaving breasts.

"That says you know me well enough to hear me out. I happen to be short on certain information, and you happen to come recommended… right?" Stuffing the note into her handbag, she gestured to an empty seat facing her. Declining the offer, he was forced to command a sharp intake of breath due to the pungent odour, made possible by a two layer cocktail of perfume and BO that wafted up to greet him from the mask of foundation rouge and exuberant mascara. "God she must walk around like that for a bet" he told himself. Rita then brought him back to reality.

"So, you got through the interview darling, what do you want from me?"

"I'm looking for the whereabouts of a certain person, who used to frequent this pub. Does the name Andy Dowling mean anything to you?" Almost immediately, Eastern sensed her body language was in tune with his enquiry, as she opened up to remonstrate.

"If we are talking about the same sicko, then yes! You bet I do. And if you happen to catch up with him you can tell the lousy scumbag that he still owes me."

"He's not exactly flavour of the month, is he sweetheart? The problem is, I'm led to believe the guy has moved on, and I need to know where to start looking."

She then retained a more positive attitude in her approach. "You might want to try the Queens Park area of Brighton. That's as good a place as any."

"Yeah you seem pretty sure of yourself…how do you figure that one out?"

Before replying, her face distorted into a knowing smile, causing Eastern to choke on his Scotch. "Experience darling, it goes with the job. Over the years I've learnt that what the majority of men speak about when they're asleep, they nearly always mean…trust me. I could write a book on the subject."

It now became Eastern's turn to smile, but in a benevolent way, as he turned to leave. "I appreciate the tip sweetheart, the next time I have a nightmare, I'll try not to think about you."

Apart from the evergreen grief arising from the traffic congestion in the city, he had every reason to feel a sense of satisfaction as he drove back to his office. "Hum, Queens Park," he mused. At least it narrowed down the picture somewhat. Assuming of course that the information turns out to be kosher. Momentarily he was forced to shudder as to its origin, when a mental image of the 'lovely Rita', suddenly invaded his subconscious.

Having taken another solemn oath to rectify his troublesome door catch, he checked his answer phone for messages. "Damn! She's obviously been in touch while I've been out…Hi Joan? Yeah it's Mike, I just picked up your call. How are things in Hove at present?" The quality of her voice alone seemed to create a subsidy for any problems he may have held. For the first time in a long while, he felt good.

"Fine thanks, just fine. In fact I've had some company. Toni my journalist friend came down from London for a couple of days, so I can't complain." She then went to say that she had been in touch with her estranged husband. He advised that there was some ready mail waiting to be collected, and that she had arranged to collect it sometime within the next 24 hours. She further went on to suggest that they arrange a meet for that evening to mull things over.

For his part, Eastern had already made the decision to keep what little information he held on ice for the time being. "Another day isn't going to make any difference," he assured himself, or so he thought. In ignorance, pertaining to a vital development he could never have foreseen, it was later left to the media circle into shocking him back into the realms of reality. His defence was, and always had been, solid and unwavering, now it was under attack. "In my line of business, and for the benefit of hindsight, I only deal in facts. Whereas tabloid headlines are a two minute reminder, intended to lull the subscriber that the rest of the news is worth reading. Only to find out 24 hours later, that they're fish and chips fodder."

He'd only bought the newspaper that same morning for something to look at, whilst awaiting an order for a Chinese takeaway for his lunch. Bearing in mind his personal and current involvement with the case, it made his intended meal seem futile in comparison as the words of the headline instantly grabbed his attention. They were bold, they were specific, and they were in his face:

POLICE CHIEF IN BUNG PROBE
'Whistle blower' stands by statement

The report went on to say that a leading tabloid had been contacted some two weeks ago with a view to running a story concerning an alleged monetary theory. The accusation revolved around a deep rooted conspiracy, existing within the ranks of one leading police force. Owing to the importance of the allegation, the instigator has not yet been identified or indeed investigated at this stage and reporting restrictions had been put in place. One particular source suggests that there is a possibility he may have held a position in the force concerned, prior to his resignation. The story cover also stated that resulting from an initial enquiry, two members of that force have subsequently been removed from their posts within the CID branch and, as a result, were currently suspended on full pay, pending a full blown internal enquiry, led by the IPCC, due to get underway shortly.

A well delivered, and proverbial, smack in the mouth would have had less impact had it been available. As it was, a cold rush of air swept over his body, gripping him like a vice. Slowly he lowered the paper, his eyes still transfixed, as he struggled to take in his worst verbal nightmare. At the same time, his blood count accelerated and threatened to turn his heart inside out. On a par, a bell the equivalent to 'Big Ben' began pounding away inside his diffused brain that was going nowhere fast. And then, a sudden breakthrough, as a clouded image of Joan took centre stage.

"That'll be £7.50 please Mike," the proprietor of the takeaway requested.

"Say what?" he hadn't yet adjusted to the situation at hand.

"Your meal of course! It's ready to go."

The ground was harder then what he thought as he came crashing down to earth, but at least he landed on the kosher side of reality.

"Sorry Ling, I was bleedin' miles away…here, keep the change mate." Tossing a £10 note on the counter, Eastern grabbed his meal. Thrusting the paper under his free arm, he hurriedly departed the shop with the appearance of a man on a mission.

The puzzled Chinese owner watched him leave and was heard to remark "He's obviously got a woman problem, I know he doesn't gamble."

Knowing his track record, the observation made was nearer the truth than could have been imagined. As ten minutes later Eastern began making a bad job of juggling a portion of spare ribs with a feverishly placed phone call. "C'mon Joan, pick up the bloody phone…ah, there you are thank God!"

"Calm down Mike, I've only been outside relaxing on the balcony, I get the impression you're uptight. There isn't a problem I hope?" It would have been so damn easy to have brushed her question to one side by saying no and passing his obvious persona off as a personality disorder. "But Joan is no ordinary client" he told himself, and pursued his original line of enquiry.

"I was wondering, have you had the chance to read this morning's paper yet , or indeed any paper come to that?"

"To be honest Mike, I haven't left the flat since breakfast, should I have done then? The papers I mean?"

"I'll get round to that in a moment Joan. My biggest concern is making sure that you're safe and well." Eastern then went on to relay his morning's progress and finished on a confident note, as to Andy Dowling's possible whereabouts.

"At least it sounds like it could turn out to be a vital lead," Joan concluded. "So what is the emphasis on the paper routine about?"

Rather than leaving her struggling with a head full of random scenarios, he agreed to meet her at the flat within the hour and summarised by stating "The case itself is beginning to get complex, so we need to hopefully draw some conclusions," and left it at that.

"Oh I see you've brought me one to read…come on in Mike." Joan indicated the paper under his arm and ushered him inside. Once he looked settled she produced a bottle of Scotch and a carafe of water, which she diligently placed on the table in front of him with an added tumbler. "I thought you might like to help yourself Mike, so relax and enjoy."

For Eastern the moment now became surreal, as a wave of sentiment swept over him. "Silly I know, but how…?"

"What?" Joan cut in.

"The label on the bottle, it's Bells. That's the only brand I drink."

"That's right," she replied coyly. "Just call it a woman's intuition." That was a nice touch he thought, but his real interest lay in the content of the newspaper which he handed to her.

"Here. This should give you something to think about Joan. Although it won't be for the right reasons I'm afraid." Nursing his Scotch, he sat back while anticipating a reaction. When, as he expected, his prophesy finally appeared, he began to witness a side of Joan that was strangely alien to him. As a result, he wasn't about to argue her case.

Coolly and calmly she tossed the paper to one side. Leaning forward on her elbows, she rested her chin onto her clenched fists.

At that moment it became clear to Eastern that Joan wasn't about to divulge her feelings at this stage, choosing instead to create a hypnotic tension, whilst her inner thoughts remained secluded and locked into a time bomb that was slowly ticking away. A mask of determination etched in pure granite, now washed over her face and in the process accentuated her high cheek bones. Her piercing ice blue eyes bored searchingly into his own, almost as if she was looking for some form of approval that lay in waiting, ready to emerge from a hidden agenda when directed.

For once in his life, Eastern had been subjected into becoming a spectator, and a dumb one at that. Forced as he was into looking on open mouthed as her unflinching gaze gave way to acting out a hungry tigress prior to making a kill. This indeed happened to be Joan Travers playing on her now pent up anger. The verbal aspect of her one woman show, rapidly ensued.

"It looks to me like judgement day has arrived too early for comfort. This isn't the way it was supposed to be Mike, the whole damn mess has blown up in my face. I'm far from being impressed, knowing that I've got more to lose than a 'bent' husband. I blame myself for not acting sooner, and knowing that with his influence, this token allegation will become yesterday's news in a week's time."

"If the system is flawed, then..." he wasn't allowed to finish.

"No Mike, let me finish. We can't let the bastard get away with this, somebody has got to see him for what he really is. Having said that, I can't afford to go public on the matter. The media circus alone would leave us far too far exposed." She broke off suddenly, to shudder in resignation. Eastern couldn't help but notice the first signs of a crack surfacing in her restrained composure.

"Take your time Joan, you're not on trial here remember," he demanded. "You didn't ask for any of this crap to happen. Right now, you need to be stronger than you have ever been. I'm sure that between us we can focus on the positives that we are aware of, rather than dwell on the uneasy 'spiel' that's beginning to emerge." To console or be consoled, that is the question. And Joan was back to her old self once again.

"I hear what you say Mike, and I guess you're right...I was wondering..."

"Go on."

"What would his take be, on this latest disclosure?"

"And him being?"

"Why Mr X of course, or rather Dowling?"

"That's an interesting question Joan, and one that we need to consider. I would like to think that if I was Dowling at the moment, I'd feel happy in knowing that I had an unexpected ally, namely our covert friend the whistleblower. As far as I'm concerned, he has saved me a lot of grief, purely on the strength of a phone call. At the moment, your husband isn't aware of our business 'arrangement' so ideally it needs to stay that way. To me, it's vital that he believes that you've been playing the loving housewife and that you know absolutely nothing about his dirty racket. Our biggest concern would be if Dowling decides to contact your husband directly. And by that I mean threaten him. If he does, you do realise that it will be game over between you and him? Plus of course, your convenient cover could be blown apart."

Staring back at him, Joan toyed with her drink glass before allowing a moment of hidden truth to surface. "In one respect, you could say that Dowling has done me a service without knowing it. Purely by chance, he has given me the opportunity to break free from a marriage that was going nowhere. Fast." It was a bold statement, and directly off the cuff, which Eastern readily took note of.

"I think I can live with that as an advantage," he was quick to assess. His thoughts then returned to the business at hand. "Before I forget Joan, you happened to mention a letter earlier on. Is it relative to our case?" Slowly she shook her head.

"I'm not totally sure what to make of it. Hang on a second." Reaching inside a nearby folder that lay on the table, she produced an unopened envelope. "Ah, here we are. I certainly don't recognise the handwriting...here...see what you make of it." Eastern scrutinised it for a few seconds before passing judgement.

"Obviously it has been posted locally or thereabouts. It has a Gatwick registration...cheap stationary...not a good sign...shall I?" He gestured as if to open it.

"By all means," Joan concurred. "I'm done with worrying." It wasn't so much what he said, or what was about to follow, or indeed the way that he said it, that really mattered. Without hesitation, he surgically ripped the envelope open and elected to let his face say it for him. In his haste to confirm the contents, he inadvertently allowed a secreted photograph to slip out from beneath his fingers.

"Damn it! I'm sorry Joan, but this arsehole just doesn't know when to stop. He's seriously beginning to piss me off again."

"There's no point in stating the obvious Mike. Let's see what the deranged creep has got to say for himself this time." The message itself was brief in content, but at the same time ensured that the reader would be left under no illusions as to its importance should they decide not to conform.

Mrs Conway

Just to remind you that I'm still on your case (thought the photo came out well). I shall expect you to contact me at precisely 8pm Wednesday night on the new number (enclosed). I'm sure that you won't let me down.

Yours, WINNER

"Going by the date, he's obviously sent this before the story broke in the paper. Blast! I can't even surmise what his reaction will be, once he does know."

"And the phone call, how do we deal with that one?"

"It's priority Joan, we have to reciprocate I'm afraid, we can't just ignore the guy. Right now, he's holding a gun of convenience at your head...think about it. The enclosed photo, and I presume it's kosher, says it all . The fact that he's obviously followed you at some stage to get a result, is damning enough."

"I'm confused, how could he have known my movements? Security wise, I've done everything by the book...you know that."

"And that, if you should choose to, is the problem. What I'm saying is, that you're a creature of habit Joan, and routine tends to rule your life. I strongly suspect that Dowling has picked up on that. And for that reason alone, he probably knows you better than you know yourself. This game that he's been playing, for want of a better word, isn't something that's happened overnight. This has been going on for weeks. The creep had had you under a microscope. By the way, is there anything you can tell me about the photo itself?"

"I presume you mean possible background...location, that sort of thing?"

"Yeah, you're catching on fast Joan...now think hard."

"I don't have to, the building behind me," she stopped and indicated with her finger. "That shop behind me next to the boutique, that's where I have my hair done."

"And the location?"

"It's in the Lanes. And that would have been taken over two weeks ago, just before I received the very first letter from him. God! It makes me shudder to think that he could have got that close to me. Saying that, I wouldn't have known what the creep looks like anyway."

"Unfortunately for us, that's the advantage he's able to work with." Eastern confirmed. "But not for long, I promise you. I intend on visiting the daily 'Argus' office, dig through their records and see what I can come up with. There's a chance I might come across a photo of Dowling, taken before and after his father's trial. My 'snout' tells me that he was a front stage activist, when the old man was sent down. So yeah, it could pay off."

"Please God" Joan replied emphatically, and went on. "Which leads me to another question."

"Which is?" Eastern enquired dubiously.

"I'm thinking supposition for a minute. To me, this whole rotten business centres around the fact that Dowling, amongst other things, is telling us that he's terminal. How can we be so sure he's telling the truth?"

"And your point being?"

"We honestly don't know. We have only got his word for it, who's to say he's only using the claim as a ploy. If so, it would put pressure on me by aiding him to obtain a quicker and efficient result. And then there's the question of compensation of course, you can't just rule that out. I'm slowly beginning to think, that our mutual friend Mr Dowling, is fast becoming one healthy but devious bastard."

Eastern was forced to chuckle, if not to take the strain out of their conversation. "You're nobody's fool Joan, I'm impressed. In fact, the possibility had crossed my mind on more than one occasion. And it certainly needs consideration."

With that thought in mind, and a genuine access to the bottle of Scotch, it became well after midnight, before an arranged cab arrived to take Eastern home. Needless to say, he slept like a baby.

Chapter Six
A snap decision

The abhorrent chemical fumes exuding from the nearby laundrette, complimented by the odious smell of Chinese cuisine, proved to be far more efficient than his alarm clock. It also reminded him, to keep his rear window shut at night. "Shit! Is that the time?... that's bloody obscene." Eastern contended, through bleary half open eyes, each one pleading to remain anonymous. Moments later, a well directed blow from his pillow resulted in the said clock taking the brunt of his frustration. "Fuck the world, I want to get off," he grunted, and promptly lost himself under his duvet.

Some two hours or so later, the world according to Eastern ground to a halt by colliding with reality. Having survived a self induced coma earlier, it was left to his mirror to analyse a body check. The inevitable shower, followed by the first cigarette of the day, suitably eased him back into the frame. "Things to do, places to go," figured highly on the day's agenda, as he sipped a debateable looking coffee. The stairs in his flat were as usual nothing less than genuine, which was more than could be said for the rush hour traffic, inhabiting Western and London road Brighton.

Exiting Preston Circus, the city was left to its own devices as he headed for the suburbs and 'Clarion House', a local newspaper publishing site. Once inside the records department, he lost no time explaining his presence. Furnished with the facts relating to the case in question, it was then left to Eastern to attempt to uncover the vital information he so desperately sought. Locating the actual press coverage, stemming from the Spelling murder, became the easy part. As were the graphics surrounding the late Henry Dowling. Unfortunately, any visuals linked to his son, appeared to be non existent. Not to be outdone, he decided to pursue another line of thought.

Aware that Dowling junior had been a past activist, when supporting his father's alleged treatment by the police, now suggested to him that the likelihood of a prosecution due to his extremism was a possibility not to be ignored. Half an hour later, his hunch proved to be conclusive, as he honed in on a reliable press cutting.

Local man bound over to keep the peace

It was never going to make front page interest, but the 'mugshot' that accompanied the report more than compensated for his own input, by giving him reason to vent off. "Sorted! You arsehole, now let's get it on!"

Sometime later, and armed with a blown up version of Dowling, he duly parked up just beyond the 'Pepper Pot' in Queens Park, opposite Islingword Road, his sole aim being to carry out a pub crawl hoping to connect a possible sighting of his nemesis. It was always going to be a long, outside shot, but a necessary one nevertheless.

'Lady luck', it seemed had chosen to take the day off in his case. Any feedback from his enquiries had proved fruitless. Spotting a 24/7 corner shop on the way back to his car, reminded him that he was low on cigarettes. Once again Eastern asked the question – it was beginning to be a bad habit. "Do you happen to recognise this person?" As expected, he drew a blank. Pocketing his cigarettes and the photo, he turned to leave.

"Hang on a minute man…maybe I was a bit too hasty." The proprietor, Eastern noted, was obviously unsettled about something. Assuming he may have been short changed, he held his hand in expectation. "No, no! The photo, something had just occurred to me, it's only a stab in the dark mind you but…"

Eastern retaliated before the man could finish. "Here. Take a really good look this time," and he thrust the photo back in the man's face.

"Yeah, that face definitely bothers me, when was it taken, any idea?"

"You're probably looking at three or four years ago."

"Only I notice that the guy has got long hair there, now what would happen if I do this I wonder?" By manipulating his hand, he endeavoured to blank out the hair on the image. Eastern could only look on in gathered interest, and moments later he wasn't disappointed as a smug look decorated the proprietor's face. "Yeah, no question about it, it was the hair that threw me at first. I recognise him now, the guy you're looking for has got a close shaven hairstyle now. He comes in here about twice a week, and stocks himself up with 'zap' food."

"Is there anything else you can tell me about him?" Eastern implored.

He shook his head, "I'm afraid not guv. To be honest, you'd get more contact out of a stuffed dummy…know what I mean?"

"He's coming across as being your typical stereotypical loner, from what you say."

"Yeah, right, except to say that he's got an attitude problem to go with it. And apart from that, it's fair to say he's local…that's about it I reckon."

Thanking him for his trouble, Eastern left the shop feeling more decisive than when he entered. With 'bullets' to fire, and a few 'maybe's' beginning to make sense, what price an address? Now that would be the business in sharing that thought. His wave of confidence was still on a roll, as he emerged suitably toned from a delayed shower that evening. Exiting his flat ten minutes later, gave him cause to vent off. "I figure the crazy bastard think he's dealing with a frightened and defenceless woman. Well, I've got news for you sunshine, welcome to the club of three!"

He was still stuffing his face with a salami bagel, via a local 'nosh' bar on the way over, as he arrived at Joan's flat. After making his excuses, Eastern lost no time in grooming Joan, regarding her premeditated call…

"Now remember Joan, it's essential that for the present you go along with any decisions he promotes. Remember this call is all about 'mind games'. Promise him everything without sounding too patronising. And try to imagine he's controlling you, that way we get more out of him. The chances are he could get too over confident and let something slip."

"What if he gets over demanding?" Joan asked hesitantly.

"Just run with it, don't forget he's telling you as it is, by not being aware of my involvement with you. Remember the pressure is all on his twisted ego, and not yours!"

"You make it all sound so convincing Mike, I hope I come across the same way."

"Trust me, you will. And rest assured that I'm listening in on the extension in the hall...good luck." The following two minute time check leading up to 8pm seemed like an eternity. Finally Joan dialled the appropriate number, after taking her lead from Eastern.

The monotonous dialling tone was beginning to have its effect on her demeanour, adding to her apprehension level. Moments later, her concern became short lived as the sought after connection became a reality. Swallowing hard, she steeled herself before speaking in a predetermined manner and addressed herself by using her married title as planned.

"This is Joan Conway speaking, can you identify yourself please?"

"Good evening Mrs Conway, congratulations on your timing. It's good to know that relationship is ongoing, even if it is at a distance. And yes, if you haven't already guessed, this is 'winner' speaking." The dulcet tone of his voice sounded natural and certainly educated, Eastern noted, but, at the same time reliant on sinister undertones as a means of conveying authority. Joan then continued where she had left off, only this time in a connived manner.

"If that is the case, I really can't see how I fit into this charade. Your grudge is with my husband surely? He's the one person you should be dealing with." Eastern was then forced to wince at her self proclaimed naivety.

"Damn it Joan! Don't push your luck...now is not the right time." Dowling then picked up where Joan had left off.

"Please, give me some credit Mrs Conway, we both know that you alone are my biggest asset in this charade, as you put it. Any communication I could or might have had with that unrelenting husband of yours would have been via a shredder. As a result, my intentions rest solely on his feelings towards you. I think I make myself perfectly clear, wouldn't you say?"

"Let is go Joan for Christ's sake before you really piss the guy off." Showing restraint while listening in was proving difficult for Eastern at this point. Fortunately, Dowling bailed him out with a fresh approach.

"Now then Mrs Conway, more importantly we need to talk about this information that I require from you, in furthering my late father's claim for justice."

"I see, having said that, you do realise that it isn't something I can obtain over night? Especially when I don't have any proof available to me."

"Good move Joan, keep kidding him along," Eastern mused. For reasons of his own, Dowling then decided a more rigid stance was required.

"Please don't take me for a fool Mrs Conway. I do happen to read the newspapers and I can change my mind quicker than I can exchange my address. I thought I made myself clear, when I said the onus was on you to deliver? In fact, I'll be generous and give you two weeks to come up with substantial evidence alluding to my father's case. In the meantime I'll take your mobile number, rather than writing to you. We wouldn't want your husband thinking that you're the flavour of the month…would we? Incidentally, they tell me that Hove is popular this time of year." Joan reluctantly handed over her mobile number. Then suddenly, without any warning, the line went silent as Dowling decided to hang up.

Minutes later, an air of anti climax clashed with intense relief ensued, as Joan opened up her heartfelt feelings. "I think I need a drink Mike, in fact make that a large one. It just might enable me to get that perverted creep out of my system."

"I'd be the last one to argue with that Joan, you've more than earned it. I thought that you handled your end well, considering what he laid on you."

"He certainly made his position clear enough. So, what did you manage to glean from our conversation, if anything?"

"Hard to say Joan, it was too one sided. Mind you…" he tailed off prematurely, to allow a nagging doubt to surface. "It's probably nothing, but the reference that Dowling made concerning a change of address; I have to say it bothers me."

"Really, in what way?"

"The emphasis alone, it came across as sounding like a half-baked threat, as opposed to a voluntary statement. I honestly don't think he meant to say it. It could imply that the word still happened to be fresh in his mind, and possibly linked to a recent association of some kind."

"But when you consider that it's only a month or so that he vacated his own flat, I can only presume that could be the unintentional link." Her analytical prognosis gave Eastern cause to smile in a calculating manner.

"In a manner of speaking, you're right, and the more I think about it, my gut feeling is telling me that the egotistic idiot might have moved back there...think about it for a minute?"

"I'm trying hard Mike, but I can't see where you're going with it."

"Hear me out, and then consider this Joan. Dowling, I believe, is thinking like a fox. I'm assuming that he's doubled back over old ground to throw us off the scent. Meaning, that the last place anyone would expect to find him at this stage..."

"...would be back living at his own flat, as you suggested." Joan interrupted, leaving Eastern to nod aggressively before continuing.

"Precisely! Now you're thinking like me Joan. The man isn't stupid, I suspect he thinks that somebody has been tailing him, and that's why he moved out in the first place. Come to think of it, his flat was still empty when I first visited it, which is unusual in itself."

"Why do you say that?" Joan questioned.

"Flats, right now are at a premium. His place would have been snapped up within minutes under normal circumstances. Which reminds me, the Hove implication isn't looking very secure. How do you feel about relocating, and changing your life style at the same time? He's managed to find you once, don't let him give us another opportunity...right?" Joan pondered for a while before committing herself.

"It would be a wrench, but it makes sense Mike, plus of course a showdown discussion with my husband. Incidentally, you need to brief me on that one, it is imperative to know what he has got planned.

Especially with the probe case hanging over him." Eastern chewed on his lip before replying.

"Amen to that." He concluded and went on." We're in no man's land at the moment and delving comes to mind. First thing tomorrow, I'll pay the caretaker a visit at Dowling's old flat – he doesn't miss a trick. In the meantime, I need you to contact your husband, and chase up some letting agents as well. I'll phone you around midday, and then we can pool what feed back what we have, if any."

Everything that could have been said was now buried. It was now time to relax. Together, they still found plenty to talk about, although the topic of conversation had nothing to do with the case. The evening finished on a high and unexpected note, much to Eastern's surprise. On arrival back at his flat that night, the suspect lock to his front door worked perfectly for the first time in months."

Chapter Seven
Food for thought

Mike Eastern's judgement on the subject of outside catering looked set for a bad day. All due to the 'culinary delights' served up by the 'OVERDONE RASHER' - that, being the media café situated opposite his flat. Having had the benefit deriving from a good night's sleep under his belt, meant that it was going to take something a little bit special to cap it off. All Eastern had to do was cross the road.

The proprietor greeted him in his own flamboyant cockney manner, as he strode in. "Morning Mike, how's life in the underworld? That bad, eh?" he took it on himself to presume. "So what's yer stomach saying mate, breakfast 'A' or 'B'?"

"What's the difference then Benny?" he quipped, "Assuming that they're both legal of course."

"Not a lot, they're both kosher, although 'B' is £1.50 cheaper on account there's less grease involved."

"In that case, I'll run with the 'B'. By the way, I don't suppose you've got a morning paper kicking around?"

"You're a bleedin' PI for God's sake. You find a clue, I've gotta business to run." As luck would have it, Eastern spotted what he'd been looking for on a nearby table. No! he hadn't missed it, Benny's debateable coffee had seen to that. A particular article on the inside page of the 'Clarion' screamed back at him.

A FURTHER SUSPENSION AS CONSPIRACY PROBE GATHERS MOMENTUM

The crime report went on to say that amongst other things, as of last night, another member of the local force, this time attached to the vice squad, had been placed on suspension pending further enquiries, bringing the total number of suspects to three. When challenged by reporters, as he was seen leaving Brighton Central this morning, DCI Conway refused to make any comment, and was driven away to HQ in an unmarked police car accompanied by his father, a Chief Constable Daniel Conway.

"There yer go mate, get yer 'Hampstead Heath' (teeth) round that little lot." Eastern's space was suddenly invaded by Benny as he arrived with his order. The latter's interest was then drawn to the conspiracy article that Eastern was reading.

"Funny old business that," he commented and motioned towards the press report.

"Uhm...?" Eastern was heavily engrossed to notice, and nodded robotically.

"The reference to the 'Old Bill', it bleedin' stinks mate, what's your take on it?" Eastern glanced upward looking a trifle fazed.

"Oh, sorry mate...I was miles away...yeah, the breakfast looks the business...thanks." A confused Benny scratched his head, and walked away muttering to himself.

Digesting the facts in the press report would have been a whole lot simpler than Benny's idea of a greaseproof breakfast, had he known Eastern's interest in the case. Foremost on his mind, as he mulled it over, would be in knowing the identify of the whistleblower. "What wouldn't I give for that?" he wondered. "Or the location of the 'safe house' he's occupying. Although in retrospect, I wouldn't give a Lottery win in exchange for that poor sucker's neck. I wonder what induced him to go public in the first place? Somebody must have really pissed him off. And nobody is saying whether he's straight or indeed if he's a member of the 'bent' brigade."

In summing up, his close run alleged legal breakfast might possibly have numbed his brain into disregarding one other vital aspect. "Credulous as it seems, who's to say that Dowling or the informant himself isn't ensnared in a bizarre double act of their own?" Food for thought would serve as a pub under the circumstances.

"I'll catch you later Benny," he called out minutes later, and exited the café. Once outside he headed for the Seven Dials, intent on checking his theory that Dowling might have been reinstated at his old flat.

Ignoring the use of the ground floor flat bell, he decided to take the steps leading down to the basement, on a whim that the caretaker was home. Eastern wasn't about to be disappointed as recognition came easy.

"I know you, don't I? You were here the other week. I wish someone would tell me what's going on, nobody tells me anything these days. He's back you know…him in flat two. He arrived a couple of days ago out of the blue. Told me that he had some business up North that needed sorting out. Poxy job, I dunno where I am."

Thus far, Eastern had opted to remain silent, as the caretaker appeared to be on a verbal roll. Eastern was now struggling to suppress his elation. Without having to ask for it, he'd just been handed the relevant information he'd craved for, on a platter. At least he wasn't short in showing his gratitude.

"Here, take this, something for your trouble. Go and buy yourself a new broom." Without any ado, he stuffed a £10 note in the man's hand. "Just one other thing, unless I call round again, you've not seen me before…got it? Oh, I almost forgot, here's my card. In the event you spot anything out of the norm, then bell me…yeah?"

"Sure guv, I get the picture. Leave it with me. Eyes and ears eh?"

"Please God" Eastern told himself and went on his way, leaving a disillusioned caretaker to wonder why anybody would want to give him £10 to buy a broom he didn't want.

On the way back to his own flat, Eastern couldn't help to disguise his good fortune in knowing Dowling had possibly blown his cover. And, as a result, was now a prime candidate for intense scrutiny 24/7 if necessary. He also reminded him that a nothing to lose call with his internal ally DS Curtis was on the cards.

"Johnnie, yeah it's Mike Eastern. I thought we might have a chat."

"Hi Mike, would that be as in shop, or is it just a courtesy call?"

"That depends on what you know that I don't. I'm interested in your elusive chief witness for the Crown."

"Isn't everybody? You should know better than to ask mate. The press of course are under orders, plus the poor bastard who's doing all the 'singing', is meanwhile wrapped up in cotton wool."

"I'll take that as a 'no' then Johnnie?"

"Good try Mike…oh, there is one thing I managed to pick up on."

"Anything…anything at all you think might help."

"Well, for what it's worth, I recently had access to a taped statement, made by the whistleblower, prior to the suspensions. You can distinctly hear him saying the word 'we' twice within a thirty minute period. I thought it sounded most odd at the time, especially as nobody else had referred to it. Since then, having heard and read other transcripts made by him, the word 'we' doesn't appear at all. It's almost as if he's corrected himself."

"I find that very interesting, and I understand how it could become vital as a possible lead. The fact 'we' is prominent, leads you to think that he's talking on behalf of himself and an unknown associate. What's your personal angle on it?"

"I'd have to say go along with it Mike, and draw what ever conclusions you can from it."

"Thanks Johnnie, it's given me something to think about, I'll be in touch."

Question, was the omission by the whistleblower a genuine one, or had he indeed made an open blunder in the heat of his initial interrogation? Eastern was still searching for the answer to the problem as his head hit the pillow later on that night.

The following morning, he was alerted by his mobile sounding off. In seconds he was on the case. "Okay Joan, that suits me fine, give me 20 minutes or so and I'll be over. We can discuss it then…yeah…bye now."

Smiling discreetly, he pocketed his mobile, after taking out a time check. There was no hiding the air of confidence in his manner.

Food for thought

"9.50am" he remarked jubilantly. "Can't be bad, normally I'd still be herding bleedin' sheep." One last look of appraisal in his mirror and a final swig of alleged coffee before he left the flat, found him heading down New Church Road in Hove.

"Hi Mike, come in. God, you didn't waste any time getting here. I hope it's for all the right reasons?" Wearing a see through lace trimmed silk negligee, Joan ushered him through to the lounge.

"There is one or two that quickly came to mind." He told himself and averted his gaze away from her negligee.

"Mike!"

"Sorry Joan I was miles away, bit early for me, saying that I could well get used to it." Ten minutes later, over a genuine coffee, Joan explained that an arranged meeting, specifically for a showdown with her husband, had now become a gilt-edged reality. When grooming her approach as to whether she declared any interest in her own precarious situation, volatile as it was, would remain vital. A hasty decision one way or another could further antagonise her current 'face off' with enigma Andy Dowling.

The short answer to that, and few other foreseeable problems, now lay directly at the feet of an unexpected force that nobody, apart from its instigator could have possibly known about. On a more positive note, Joan went on to say that she had been successful in securing fresh accommodation, namely a larger flat located in the 'village' (a pseudonym for Brunswick Square). It was available for occupation in a week's time. For his part, Eastern lost no time in divulging the fact that their dual hunch had indeed come home to roost, and ensuring that Dowling was no longer untouchable.

How far that assumption extended to, needed to be clarified. And chasing shadows wasn't what he was getting paid for. In the end, it was left to DC Curtis to take the brunt of his frustration, following a call.

"Hi Johnnie, it's me again."

"Blimey Mike, this is getting to be a habit, you'll be requesting an enrolment form at this rate."

"No bloody way mate, besides it doesn't pay enough," he quipped and went on. "Listen I thought you might be interested to learn, seeing as you're on the case indirectly, that I've managed to pin Andy Dowling down at last. Bearing in mind my clients enforced involvement with the guy, does that give you enough to bring him in?" His response wasn't what Eastern expected.

"Most unlikely mate, verbal threats only rank as hearsay as you know, and assumption doesn't wash I'm afraid."

"And the letters that she's received, that must count for something?"

"Once again no, he'll just deny everything. Besides which, how do you know that he wrote them anyway?"

"It was worth a try Johnnie, thanks anyway…be in touch." What had started on a high note now looked like turning into a shit day at the office. That is until Joan suggested they might listen to the Southern Radio news, over a spontaneous lunch invitation. In retrospect her timing turned out to be faultless. And the outcome itself, explosive as they struggled to take in the consequences arising from a situation that was rapidly spiralling out of control. The news flash that broke was as follows:

A report issued by a police press spokesperson earlier on today, has confirmed that a high ranking police officer attached to the crime squad in the city has been arrested and charged with conspiracy to pervert the course of justice. This now brings the total of arrests to four, although earlier reports coming in fear that more could be imminent. The officer, who has not yet been named for legal reasons, had been targeted following an internal investigation by the IPCC. He is now on remand to appear before Brighton Magistrates tomorrow morning, where he will be formally charged. Reporting restrictions have been lifted and full coverage will now be available as fresh reports come in.

Momentarily, a stony silence ensued, before Eastern finally decided to turn the radio off. Meanwhile, Joan's face remained expressionless. A bolt from the blue would have had less effect on her, as she endeavoured to come to terms with the situation. Instinctively, Eastern matched her gaze in a sympathetic gesture, before she returned to a form of normality. From the off, Joan appeared to be reluctant to converse, leaving Eastern to break the deadlock.

"I'm so sorry you had to listen to that, although we were both aware it would only be a matter of time before his luck ran out. But it doesn't make your position any easier in knowing that, I'm afraid."

"I've been dreading this moment Mike. That bastard has put my life through the wringer these last few months...I'm sorry...I..."

"Don't be!" he expounded. "You're the victim here remember. If you can handle this much Joan, then you will get through this. I promise you." His persuasive and direct manner seemed to have an immediate effect on her. In no time at all, Joan regained her natural composure.

"You're right of course Mike, although Dowling isn't going to be too impressed, once the report becomes official, is he?"

Eastern was quick to sense her implication. Realising that Dowling could now be subjected to more pressure to gain the one thing that was paramount in controlling his manic desire, for personal retribution. All the time Conway senior was an outside player in the charade. He held that one chance (slim as it was) to cajole if need be, a confession of sorts from him, and therefore legitimise Dowling's claim to his father's innocence.

The plain fact was, that as from now, Conway could well find himself 'banged up' indefinitely, would only ensure in severing the one link that Dowling was banking on. As a result, somebody was going to have to pay dearly for the inconvenience. And Joan, through ill-timed circumstances, had now become the 'fall guy' in taking whatever mode of revenge his maniacal personal desired. "The sooner you vacate this place, the better I'll feel." Eastern declared, and remained insistent. "Promise me that you'll book into a hotel, at least until the other flat is ready. In the meantime, I'll do a random stakeout on Dowling's place at the Dials...saying that, I'd love five minutes free time in there. It would be an opportunity to put myself about, now that would be an education. Yeah, I guess I'm going to have to work on that caretaker again. Yeah, I figure he's ripe for another backhander."

Apart from the conspiracy case continually hugging the news, the next few days were proving to be negative, in terms of investigative momentum. Surviving on a staple diet of donuts, burgers and stewed coffee for 48 hours while on a stake out did little to convince Eastern that Dowling had indeed become a physical threat. On the flip side, he felt convinced that his own well being had now entered the first stages of inheriting a duodenal ulcer. Moreover, since his pre-planned move back to his original flat, Dowling had been seduced into playing the role of an unconditional hermit, only surfacing to obtain a morning paper. Fortunately for Eastern, with 'lady luck' in the ascendancy, this particular morning began to look favourable. At around 8.30am, Dowling finally emerged on cue, only this time, he appeared to be suitably dressed.

Once again Eastern checked his watch. "Please God he's on his way into town. Ten poxy minutes, that's all I need in that bolthole of his." He emphasised. He kept Dowling in his observation up until he boarded a bus heading for Queens Road. Show time was at a premium in the stock market and Eastern wasn't about to contemplate, there being a loss on his behalf. To increase his assets would entail a further deposit, should he intend to make a 'killing' (secure information) via the sticky hands of the 'broomstick' caretaker.

"C'mon…c'mon…where the bleedin' hell are you?" His woeful patience appeared to be thinner than a razor edge, as he repeatedly took it out on the door.

By now, his intimidating patience began to get rattled, on a par with the door he was banging on. Then, without warning, his fist met fresh air, as the door suddenly flew open, to reveal the dishevelled caretaker attempting to hold his trousers up. Momentarily he was taken aback. "Can't a man even have a …." Hesitating he stopped dead in his tracks, and expressed a double take before committing himself. "Oh, it's you I see, I was just about to say I…" Eastern nodded robotically, and swiftly dismissed any lurking conclusions with a wave of his hand.

"Yeah…yeah…forget that. Now listen, I need a favour and you look like you need the money. How would you like to invest in two more brooms?" His timely offer seemed to hit the caretaker between the eyes, consequently igniting his brain into thinking he was smart.

"Why not? I bought one before as you suggested mate, I suppose I could always use another two." By now, the grin on Eastern's face was in full flight, as it met up wit his ears.

"Now you're talking sense, you're nobody's fool I can see that." He replied in an exaggerated and patronising manner and proceeded to wave some folded money in front of him. "Here, take this pony (£25) for your trouble. All I need in return is access to flat two, just for a short while." He assured him. "Now that wasn't too hard was it?" At this point, the dizzy caretaker appeared to be totally lost in translation as the inducement changed hands and continually muttered 'brooms' to himself as he fumbled in his pocket for a pass key, which he duly handed over.

"Oh, and one other thing my friend, before I forget." Eastern added. "In the event that Dowling should make an appearance, I need to be the first to know…right?"

Once inside the flat, Eastern lost no time in getting busy. Almost immediately, his eyes fell on a phone in the sparsely fitted lounge. Like a magnet it drew him in. His main interest then became focused on a note pad that lay beside it. Flicking systematically through the pages, it soon became apparent that one contact number in particular remained prominent, which, in turn, encompassed various dates and 'meet' times. The information was then secreted internally via his mobile. The dates themselves he noted stretched back some three months previous. In each case, two words 'must contact' were affixed, and plainly highlighted by means of underlining. The exposed top page then came under a secondary scrutiny, as further possible information caught his attention. Further investigation revealed that there were signs of heavy indentation. This he deduced was made from a previously written note or letter. Pocketing the page in question, he then made his way into the bedroom. Based on past experience aligned with the case history, had left Eastern in no doubts, as to what he could possibly expect to find once inside.

One wall in particular screamed out for intense examination, if only for pure unadulterated interest. From floor to ceiling, the entire area resembling a huge tabloid collateral consisting of unlimited press cuttings, mainly dating back to Dowling's late father's trial, and the aftermath relating to the latter's suicide. On a spar, and to his rising alarm, Eastern couldn't fail to spot a gallery of recognisable photos, portraying the Conway family. It soon became clear to him that they had been taken in recent months.

Time was running short, Eastern felt convinced now that he'd seen enough, leaving any conclusions he may have held for a later date. Armed with the required information, he once again pursued the caretaker. "It was nice doing business with you, here's the key, and remember if you ever need another broom…phone me."

Once installed in his own flat, Eastern lost no time in contacting DC Curtis. "Johnnie? Yeah, it's Mike. Listen, I've been privy to some information that could be of vital interest in the Dowling saga. If my hunch is right, it could turn the whole case on its head if it's kosher of course. But it will mean getting forensics involved to make that happen…what d'ye say?"

Thinking and believing is one matter, attempting to convince somebody that your theory holds water is another league apart. As usual, Curtis became the 'fall guy' and reluctantly caved in.

"This is the last time Mike, if I was a bleedin' cat I'd have more lives than a litter. I just hope that for your sake, you get a result." The combined smile and relief registered on Eastern's face, as he replaced it, said it all.

Having rested his case, he sat back and mulled over his belief that the notepaper he'd managed to purloin from Dowling's face did indeed contain a link between the latter and the would-be whistleblower. "If my logic is right," he told himself, "Then the feedback arising from the information would become priceless by exposing a conspiracy scam on the one hand, and on the other, blow the whistleblower's integrity clean out of the water in knowing he's the chief witness for the Crown prosecution. In spite of DCI Conway's emerging guilt in the scenario."

Confident as he could be, Eastern wisely bowed to supposition by concluding: "Who gives a toss anyway? It won't be over until the 'fat lady sings' anyway." Except to say that the 'lady' in this particular case, could well be the edged Crown witness. At least wheels were now turning on his behalf. Although the legal wheels it was fair to say, held the advantage on impetus, manifested by the local 'Clarion', that evening. The statement that was issued revolved around a trial date, set for five weeks' time and deriving from a second hearing, bail was once again formally rejected per se.

Food for thought

It's true to say, that midway between dicing with breakfast 'B' in the 'OVERDONE RASHER', any form of interruption would well have been classed as a reprieve. In Eastern's case, it came via an impromptu call on his mobile some 48 hours later. "Thank Christ for that!" he told himself, "I swear that bacon I've just eaten originated from a rhino's arse. Hi Johnnie, what's occurring mate? I could use something kosher right now."

"As it happens," came back the reply. "This could be your lucky day Mike. As we speak, I'm looking at the forensic report on that notepaper you sent to me…very interesting. You know me mate, I can be a cynical bastard when I have to be at the best of times. And for that reason, coincidences tend to me to be a reality." Eastern tightened his grip on his mobile in anticipation of the result.

"I could use anything right now, saying that, what have you got for me?"

"Bit of a mixed bag as it goes Mike. But get this, the report itself highlights the fact that they've managed to expose a set of initials." For a second Eastern was lost for words as he struggled to contain himself and the mere thought that his scam theory at one point could be found hovering on conjecture on his part now released visible signs that just maybe he'd got it right all along.

"No shit, and I wager they could tell a story." He was hedging somewhat, to hopefully cloud over his relief.

"Yeah, right! Exactly my sentiments Mike. So, naturally, I did a bit of digging around myself."

"And?"

"Would you believe that the initials in question corresponded with those of the whistleblower when matched? Try getting that around your head." A sustained silence ensued as Eastern gathered his thoughts. "Mike, hello? Are you there Mike? I was just…"

"Yeah…sorry mate." Eastern cut in. "Fucksake! I knew I was on to something big. Everything seems to be falling into place."

"Based on what's available, I have to agree Mike. But why do I get the feeling that you know something I don't? At worse let me consider what you've got." Eastern kept talking long enough to accept the fact that his half eaten breakfast was now cold.

"That has to be a result in itself," he grated. Curtis then readily brought him back down to earth.

"That's one hell of an assumption mate, and I can't fault your logic behind it…"

"But proving it, is something else…I know." Eastern interjected. "But trust me, I'll give it my best shot. In the meantime, I still have that suspect phone number belonging to Dowling that I need to check out. So until I know different, it's anybody's guess. I'll be in touch." His thoughts were then scuttled as Benny the proprietor began to hover.

"You gotta problem Mike? You've left more than you've eaten."

"Problem? Not as big as yours is Benny," and he looked at the bacon. "I recommend you get yourself a good brief, I've had it on good authority that there's a half demented rhino on the loose with half its poxy arse missing…know what I mean?" Shelving his mobile while grinning like a Cheshire cat, Eastern made his way out of the café, leaving Benny with his thought for the day.

Chapter Eight
An unexpected 'accident'

Eastern decided to hang on for as long as he could. Unfortunately, his mobile had other ideas and refused to play ball. "Damn!" he expressed along with his concern and frustration. "Could be that she's driving," he consoled himself. "I'll text Joan a message anyway."

Hi Joan it's important that we meet up tonight say at yours about 8. Dinner's on me.

Relaxing in a 'his and hers' cubicle while in a renowned restaurant with a client that would grace any catwalk with a wedge (roll of money) later on that same evening resulted in a business therapy he could only have dreamt about two months previous. "Please God it's infectious, I could get used to this," became one channel of thought, until an impromptu vision of the 'OVERDONE RASHER' attempted to make a guest appearance by gate crashing his space.

The feral illusion, swiftly evaporated into oblivion, due to the presence of a large medium cooked 'T' bone steak delicately placed in front of him. From then on, a cocktail of culinary delights and business acumen, made for a successful evening and terminated afterwards at Joan's retreat in Brunswick Square, over a late coffee. The quality of their conversation ranged from possible case scenarios to an outspoken admission by Joan regarding her personal life.

"As I stated before Joan, if I can establish a concrete link between Dowling and the Crown witness, the police will be forced to accept my theory. Hopefully by making a case, they will have enough information to arrest Dowling. Then we can all relax, and you especially can move on, in knowing that you'll then be safe."

"Tomorrow won't be soon enough for me Mike. Incidentally I've arranged an appointment with my solicitor on Tuesday. I've decided to file for divorce. My life until now has been a complete and utter sham, I just want out." Eastern hid his welcome relief at her admission behind a discreet smile before speaking.

"Under the circumstances, it shouldn't be a long and drawn out case. But, we wouldn't want to mar a good night by debating that." They continued to exchange pleasantries into the early hours, before Eastern rang for a cab. But not before another dinner date became a statistic. Only this time, it would strictly enhance pleasure.

The following morning, Eastern could be found up and about, and ready to 'kick arse', Even Benny's tea had that certain je ne sais quois taste about it , which was more than Eastern could say for the 'OVERDONE RASHER'. Monday morning dawned and yours truly could be found rapt in concentration as he studied the alien phone number he'd retrieved from Dowling's flat. The correlation surrounding the digits seemed to hypnotise him somewhat as he struggled to make some leeway into discovering the possibilities that lay behind them.

It wasn't as if the random numbers were going anywhere, unfortunately that was the crux of the matter. "If only you babies could talk," he muttered, in a disconsolate vein. "That way we can all go home." As an interested observer it was left to Benny to intervene and hopefully call time on any wishful thinking.

"Look at yer, grief and more grief…I dunno why you don't get yourself a 9 to 5 job like everybody else." In the end, Benny's prime intervention proved to be a good call. Mike Eastern had heard and seen enough, the urge to get busy far outweighed the prospect of downing another alleged coffee.

"Yeah, yeah, you're right of course mate. That way, I wouldn't have to put my solicitor on hold every time I want to come in here to eat… I'll see you around." Smiling broadly he exited the café, consumed with the air akin to a man on a mission. It was local, it was certainly convenient, and it was a public library. Armed with a short list of names compiled of ex policemen going back 18 months, Eastern was on course once more, intent on pursuing the source of the enigma phone number. Surrounded by enquiry books, he endeavoured to match the said number to anyone of six names on his list. It was never going to be an easy task due to the many combinations arising from the inclusion of various other home county listings.

An hour later, with two potential names still under scrutiny, his persistence finally paid dividends when the lead that he so desperately sought finally materialised. He was now in a position to ascertain that the initials as supplied by DS Curtis and verified by forensic belonged to one DC Terry Bryant, who it seems, resigned some six months previous regarding a personal matter. His last known address discovered could be found located in the Green Acres district of Shoreham. For the third time, Eastern checked the number secured on his mobile. No, he had no reason to think otherwise. Once more, Eastern heaved a sigh of welcome relief in knowing that his scam theory was undoubtedly beginning to look more kosher by the minute. Although containing his one man assassination would be hard to prove otherwise, as it was secreted in the hallowed walls of a reading room while under orders, proved to be a library too far.

Later that evening, Eastern bit his tongue while in the company of a compatible bottle of Scotch. It was apparent that at some point he'd need to physically check the number out. Ignorant of the whistleblower's domestic standing, plus the fact that he was secure in a safe house anyway meant that the chances of a verbal connection were looking extremely slim.

The time had come to act. Brimming with trepidation having dialled the number, Eastern eased himself back into a mood of uncertainty, and waited for a reaction. Within seconds he was left in no doubt as to what had transpired as the histrionic tones emerging from a familiar voice could be heard. The number that you are dialling has not been recognised due to it no longer being in service. Please hang up. It was almost as if he'd been aware, that the outcome had been a foregone conclusion. Looking unperturbed, Eastern pocketed his mobile and sought consolation in the form of a large Scotch.

"In it to win it!" became his prime thinking. Shrugging his shoulders, he momentarily allowed a streak of misplaced egotism to venture inside his reasoning. Foremost on his agenda was adjudged to be 'Mr Big', closely followed by DCI Conway. Downing the remnants in his glass, he vented his feelings. "Enjoy your freedom while you can, you'll both be history soon. And my only regret is that you will never know who put you away, but happily I can live with that!"

Loaded with confidence is one thing, but having hindsight is exclusive. In his case, Eastern could have saved his breath for the right reasons had he known there and then that at least one person's naïve persona could be found to be nearing its sell by date. On the flipside, DS Curtis was in a jubilant mood, having taken on board the admissible evidence linking Dowling to the inconceivable Terry Bryant, aka the whistleblower.

"I'm glad you called me Mike, there's no doubt in my mind and I strongly feel that my senior colleagues will undoubtedly think the same. From where I'm standing, there's definitely a case to be made. In the meantime, we need to expand our resources to find out what their co-joined conspiracy consisted of. This fresh evidence has put a whole new complexion on the original case. The way that things are happening, I can personally see this making Court 1 at the 'Old Bailey'.

"No shit? Better late than never I'm hoping. Only remember to keep me up to speed on any breakthrough mate. Meanwhile, that nutter Dowling is still on a walk about, and not forgetting of course that I've got a special client that I need to consider."

For the first time in a long while, Eastern was content to sit back and readily savour his 'poison' as opposed to utilizing his Scotch, as a means to a mouthwash. "You don't get too many positive days to the pound as of late." He mused, in a carefree manner, and shifted his gaze toward an adjacent open window. He readily noted that the normally cold stark and drab looking viaduct he'd inherited as a backdrop had now taken on a significant change in aspect. Prominent being the last of the evening sunlight chasing a thousand shadows through and around the giant archways. Even the ever present combined odour of service fumes and aromatic smells exuding from a cosmopolitan catering hive of industry, had given rise to a lightening makeover, by coming across as tolerable.

On a high one minute, and then low on the next if stated quickly, doesn't amount to much, depending on the emphasis you put on it of course. In this particular case, Eastern was gifted with the impact from what was to come, by way of his shoulders in sympathy with the word low. On top of that, the bonus emerging from a good night's sleep obliterated on demand, as he surveyed the front page of the 'Clarion' the following morning. Seconds later he would have readily settled for a smack in the mouth, should it be an option, as he strove to take in the blaring headlines

SUDDEN DEATH OF PRIME WITNESS
Police conspiracy case once again shrouded in latest mystery

"This has to be somebody's idea of a poxy sick joke…the guy has been secreted in a 'safe house' for fucksake" was his initial reaction before reading on. Due to the lack of information contained in the report the coverage he noted, was therefore not very explicit in terms of timing and conclusions, but finished by stating:

A full Post Mortem would be carried out later today, and the Coroner has been informed. The police will be issuing a further statement later, as fresh information comes to light.

Numbed by anger and acute frustration as the relevance of the witness's death hit home had now left Eastern feeling morally devastated. "Curtis…I seriously need to contact Curtis." After a few futile attempts to get through, he finally succeeded in pinning him down. The feedback he received was no different than he had anticipated.

"I don't need convincing Mike, I can fully understand how you feel respecting your personal interest in the case. But on a personal level, I'm gutted as well. In fact the team as a whole are pissed off. When I think back, we were that close to obtaining a result, and then the poor bastard goes and dies on us."

"I appreciate your loyalty Johnnie, although I still can't get my head around it all the same. One thing is for sure though. I'd give anything to be a fly on the wall in the path lab when they're doing the business...know what I mean?"

"If I didn't know you better Mike, I'd have to say I'm beginning to get the distinct impression that you don't believe his death was kosher."

"Do you?"

"I'll take a rain check on that one until the lab report becomes official. But that's not to say that I haven't got reservations of my own. I mean, there's a few 'faces' I could name who had a hell of a lot to lose before this happened..."

"And still could have." Eastern interjected strongly, and continued, "You wouldn't want to make a book on this case going away quietly. It's far too bloody clinical for my money, know what I mean?"

"Sure I do, and for two good reasons alone. One being that without the witness there's a good chance that the case as a whole could fold. In which case, certain people could and would come out of this smelling of bleedin' roses!"

"It makes me want to reach just to contemplate it. You know and I know that arsehole Conway and the little 'firm' he's surrounded by are as bent as a £3 coin."

"Point taken, but it's early days yet Mike." Curtis reminded him. "So I wouldn't dwell too strongly on it. Right now, if I were you, I'd give Dowling some priority." Together they then went on to discuss the case at various levels before Curtis pulled the plug on an intriguing conversation.

His watch was saying 10am as he left his office. Eastern opted for common sense in knowing that the parking in the village would be a problem. "Brunswick Square mate...Western Road end thanks." Acting on a whim, he had decided to call on Joan. He was still on a high as he paid the cab off. Fortunately she was in, and made no secret at being relieved to see him.

"I appreciate you calling in on me Mike, and before you say anything, I heard the news on Southern Sound, although I wish I hadn't now. I couldn't even hazard a guess as to where my position lies at this moment in time. I mean, this changes everything, doesn't it?" Eastern was having none of it.

"I won't allow a shower like that to rain on my parade, or yours for that matter Joan." He assured her. Leaning forward he grasped her shoulders tenderly. "Joan, now listen to me, in reality nothing has changed. In spite of what's happened, your husband is, and always will remain a bent cop. And again I say, nothing is going to alter that fact. The only problem as I see it, will be one of timing when proving that he isn't. But, as things stand, the only winner if there is one to come out of this unholy mess is Dowling. With the prime witness out of the frame, we'll never know if the two were ever linked to a conspiracy or not. Meaning that the heat is off him at the moment." He hesitated, to allow a positive thought to make its mark. "Apart from what I want to shift his way of course."

Releasing his grip on her, he motioned towards the nearest chair and indicated for her to sit down. "I don't know about you Joan, and I realise it's early, but I think we could both use a drink. Saying that, drink is like the poxy weather, you don't know what you're getting from one day to the next. But right now, it's raining bloody grief."

A couple of hours later, a chilled out Eastern made his way back to his flat. Strangely enough, even the enigmatic lock on his door seemed to maintain its spontaneous revival.

His five minute break from obscurity to normality was once again threatened by a chain of events, fuelled by a police press report some 48 hours later. This in turn was subsequently capitalized on by the tabloids. Devoid of any cynicism Eastern's take on the outcome of the whistleblower's Post Mortem would simply have been 'I told you so', and left it at that. The importance of why he would suggest that would probably amount to being on a par with the main air vent outlet, on the nearby launderette.

His face remained motionless, as the headlines offered up by the 'Clarion' slowly filtered through to his brain. His overall impressions based on the report could well leave him relegated to the wilderness, simply by the enormity that the case as a whole now had to offer his ongoing dilemma now embraced a verbal coupe de grace.

CHIEF WITNESS MURDERED

Conclusive evidence revealed by the autopsy. The sudden and unexplained death of the leading crown witness in the police bung conspiracy case three days ago. The victim has now been named as one Terry Bryant, a 46 year old ex DC, who was attached to the same division some six months previous, while residing at Shoreham. It has now been clarified that his reason for terminating his career arose from an ongoing internal problem. This in turn, led to his prime role in the forthcoming trial. It has been revealed that his death had been caused by asphyxiation consistent with being smothered by means of a pillow by a person, or persons, unknown. The fact that the victim was secured in a 'safe house' at the time of his death has increased the original enquiry, set up by the IPCC. The four security officers brought in by police to contain his welfare are now on full suspension as enquiries continue. No charges are being pressed at this stage. At a recent police press report, the Chief Constable, Sir Daniel Conway, father of the accused DCI Conway, was asked by a reporter for his view on his son's role in the investigation and his subsequent internment. He replied 'no comment' and stalked off. We can also disclose that an anonymous phone call received yesterday stated that up until his release Bryant was a keen and ambitious officer who would have gone far. A provisional date for his funeral has now been announced and is likely to be held in a week's time at Brighton crematorium. All relatives have now been informed.

Eastern chose to remain silent for a while as he gathered the remnants of his thoughts. The only clue to his belated foregone conclusion could now be found locked in the firmness of his voice. When he finally got round to speaking, he surmised "It would seem that my original estimation concerning the smell was way out. I can only suggest that the stink involved is getting stronger by the minute."

Later on that evening, he picked up a call made to his mobile.

"Mr Eastern?...Uhm...it's me." Although unrecognisable at first, he did detect a note of desperation in his voice.

"Does 'me' have a name?" He responded. "It usually works better that way."

"You said to call you if…" And then the penny dropped, and 'me' instantly became hot property by Eastern's standards.

"Mr Caretaker I presume? Eastern speaking, what's on your mind?"

"It's about our friend…you know…Dowling in flat two. I thought you needed to know what's occurring?"

"Well you got that bit right. So, what's going down?" The man then said that he'd spotted Dowling that same day putting two large suitcases into a hire car. He went on to say that he'd managed to take down the company's contact number. An elated Eastern thanked him for the information and assured him that another 'broom' would be in the offing soon.

Slowly and methodically he replaced the handset and looked up. As if by demand, he caught his profile in a nearby mirror. A voluntary smile had now captivated his face and he felt good. Deep inside his subconscious, a plug of well being exploded, with the velocity of an over heated gas cylinder. And in doing so, released the internal mental crap he'd been harbouring to drain away into obscurity. He continued to study his reflection in an alienable manner before nodding in a meaningful way.

And then the truth came out. "It's been a funny old day…one door shuts…and another one opens," was all he said. He was still smiling as he poured himself another Scotch. Although this one would be different from the usual, it was one that he could savour. Ten minutes later he contacted Joan.

Chapter Nine
A neighbour from Hell

"Help yourself to another drink Mike when you feel like it, you know where it is by now," Joan could be found acting out her hostess mode, in her usual conventional manner. It came at the end of a day completely addled by more revelations than the 'good book' itself. For his part, Eastern was eager to make conversation. At worse, it would be a move in the right direction, if only to detract from the latest tabloid splash.

"One thing that we can depend on Joan is knowing the whereabouts of that weasel Dowling, this time around. I've checked the company number out so first thing tomorrow I intend on paying the 'Excelsior' booking office a visit. I've been given an approximate time that Dowling was picked up today, so obtaining a drop off address shouldn't be much of an obstacle. Besides, I know the cab owner from way back, him being a past client."

"Is there anybody that you don't know Mike?" She taunted him in a sexy manner. In ignorance of his past lifestyle she would have been at a loss even if the truth had have been etched in granite! In return, Eastern was forced to bite the bullet.

"Never cut off the hand that feeds you…that's business, end of" he quickly reminded himself. "Even though she's one classy bitch," he added. Besides, he'd tested the water three times before at a cost. One more transgression could mean drowning in a sea of obscurity.

A neighbour from Hell.

Shortly after 9am the next day morning he parked up a side street leading off Dyke Road, with the intention of securing a lead into Dowling's latest and spontaneous address. Ten hectic minutes later, shortly after leaving the cab office, he soon became a statistic having been caught up in the intensity of the morning rush hour. Although the grief arising from the traffic problem would only be a blip, compared to what he had in mind, or, in fact, to where he was now heading. It made sense to turn off Western Road and use Preston Street as a shorter means of access, if and when entering the bottom end of Brunswick Square.

He slowed down to a crawl, enabling him to stare intently at each of the terraced units in turn. His body stiffened as one brass plate in particular drew him like an obsessed magnet forcing him to slam on his brakes. The sudden aura and magnitude given out by the building seemed to consume his body causing him to shudder involuntarily, as a wave of cold air swept over his body akin to a controlled Tsunami. And yet he was sweating. A recipe of disbelief and outright anger formed the core of his present state. Once again he checked the number on the brass plate. No! He was adamant that he hadn't got it wrong. It had checked out with the number handed to him by the cab company.

"This has to be bleedin' crazy, if my information is kosher." Seemed to be the best result he could apply, before his brain made an appearance. Every aspect of the building could be found stamped firmly in his memory, as he drove in a daze to the top end of the square, finally coming to a halt at Joan's apartment two minutes later.

"Calm down Mike! You're not making any sense. It's not even 9.30am and you're talking in riddles. I honestly done know where you're coming from." One very confused lady, enter Mike Eastern. He was making a lousy job of convincing her that her unbiased entry into the 'hall of frame' was now at less odds than a Jewish bacon bagel. Even the see through negligee she was wearing had failed to impress him after she readily opened the door for him. "But business is business" he once again reminded himself.

"Besides," he told himself. "Once you've seen one pussy, you've seen the lot. The only difference is that some cost more to keep than others." As he would quote, and as a past historian on the subject, he wasn't in a position to argue. In knowing that Joan's nemesis could now possibly be cosied up nearby through unbelievable circumstances and residing in a flat that it would take less time to get to than a 'quickie' divorce. Under the circumstances, Joan's approach to this latest and bizarre twist which nobody could have predicted even had Eastern coming up for air.

"This isn't a bloody game of I win, you lose, Joan. You need to get real, because the first prize could well be a blasted coffin," he insisted. While Joan accepted the fact, she was unwittingly prepared to make a stand.

"I'm sorry Mike, and I hear what you say, only this time I'm staying put." She retaliated, then continued, "I don't intend on giving that sad bastard the satisfaction of knowing that he's controlling my life... that's just how it is."

A brief stand off manifested itself, allowing Eastern to collect his thoughts. "I'm sorry too Joan, it's become plain to see that I can't persuade you to leave. Having said that, I admire the 'chutzpah' in you. Nevertheless, the fact that you're living on your own is a concern and it bothers me, as you well know."

"It doesn't have to be like that you know." She replied casually.

"Meaning?" What followed next, including the intense impact it made, was nothing short of swallowing an unexploded hand grenade. Her reply, when it came, was coordinated to perfection.

"I'm saying Mike that you could always move in with me."

It was one hell of a decision to lay on somebody when familiar with their current disposition. For his part, Eastern felt himself being metaphorically torn apart. Momentarily, his confused mind swayed from the convenience of a luxury apartment and onwards to a vision of the 'OVERDONE RASHER'. And, not forgetting, the viaduct tapestry that went with his zero rated bed sit. As you can imagine, it was a close run decision to make!

He smiled in defeat, and shook his head likewise. "I guess you win Joan, although we do need to make some ground rules around here... right?"

And so it was settled. Eastern spent the next couple of days relocating, before deciding to find out whether or not Dowling had a liking for fresh air. The park bench situated on the green adjacent to the latter's latest bolthole became a blessing in disguise, leaving Eastern to take full advantage of it. Although, even at this stage, he couldn't be totally sure Dowling's move was more than a temporary one.

On this particular day, and having secured a midday 'Argus' newspaper, he made the bench his own, and hopefully Dowling's space thrown in. Aware as he could be at the time he failed to note the report at first glance, mainly because it took up a slot in the stop press 'breaking' news.

SECURITY GUARD CHARGED WITH CONSPIRACY TO MURDER WHISTLEBLOWER IN BUNG CASE

On a whim, Eastern was sorely tempted to contact DS Curtis for more information, but then reneged in knowing that his position in the queue would be a valid one. Some thirty minutes later, his thoughts were justified. Curtis was in his face explaining the details surrounding the arrest, and the varied conclusions therein.

"No, nothing about this case surprises me anymore Johnnie," was his opening gambit. He continued to probe, "How big a conspiracy in your opinion, are we talking about mate?" he ventured.

"The size, as you put it, is irrelevant Mike in terms of physical. It's the importance of 'Mr Big' alone that is paramount. Without doubt, he is our prime concern to us. Whoever sanctioned Bryant's murder has to carry a whole lot of clout…do you agree?"

"Absolutely."

"And just to make matters worse, I figure that the arsehole responsible is in our own backyard."

"Yeah, well I'd have put money on that you were going to say that. I've been thinking along those lines myself for some time now."

"Exactly, any other scenario doesn't even warrant a motive. Anyway, for what it's worth, the guard we're holding in custody at the moment is keeping 'schtum'. We figure he's only a pawn within a major organisation anyway. And it's early days of course. Given time, I feel certain that he will crack eventually, and allow the flood gates to open."

Eastern thanked him for his time and information, and passed on Dowling's new address at the same time. Later on that evening, Joan happened to receive a cold phone call. The consequence of which brought her back into the realms of reality. At the time it came through, she happened to be on her own. Meanwhile, Eastern was in the process of paying Dowling's old flat a visit. Their conversation went:

"Mrs Conway? This is 'winner' speaking as promised. I'm rather hoping that you may have some fresh news for me, and before you say it, I too read the papers. Strange isn't it? How a person's situation can go from a to z in such a short space of time. I wonder what your husband is thinking about right now? At least his time won't be wasted, in knowing that every day for the rest of his life will become one long habitual routine. The best part of it, I hasten to add, spent in solitude assuming that he's not 'got at' first of course. A 'bent' cop on the inside is only one rung away from a nonce. So I'll leave you to think about his future. I'll leave you to work that one out."

"If that's the case," she retorted. "Then I fail to see what type of satisfaction you would want from me?" The exclusive stance that she had taken then continued in the same vein. "You have to believe that my marriage died a death months ago. Like yourself, I also happen to be a victim of circumstances. As things stand now, there is no way that I could influence my estranged husband's judgement on your terms. I'll leave that for the courts to decide. One other thing, as from now, this number will no longer be recognised."

Satisfied that her fresh approach with regard to her own standing would remain intact per se, Joan took the initiative and promptly hung up. The moment he walked through the door and sounded her body language out, Mike's instinct took control.

"If you've got a problem Joan, I suggest that we talk about it. You know the rules."

Reluctantly she allowed her face to drop. "It's that obvious is it?"

Eastern offered up a jocular smile before replying. "Putting it mildly, it's not exactly 'Oscar' season, so why don't you start from the beginning?" Ten minutes later his present mood had swung like an out of date pendulum. "Damn it Joan, you say that you actually hung up on him? I blame myself, I should have been here. That was not a good move Joan." Shrugging his concern to one side, she went on to explain that she was intending to ditch her mobile. And hopefully by doing so, it would switch the onus on to Dowling, and all the blame and grief that goes with it.

"Don't let's forget Mike, that as things stand, we know where my husband is this time around. And right now…" she contested strongly, "I could be anywhere and he wouldn't know." Eastern was forced then to cave into her logic but with reservations.

"Reverse psychology is one thing Joan, but unless you've forgotten, we are dealing here with an 18ct nutter, who is now holed up less than a breath away. I mean, how surreal is that?"

In spite of Eastern's good intentions, Joan chose to remain persistent by throwing caution to the wind. "His rotten choice, not mine! Me? I'm through with running. The sooner he's out of my life then so much the better." She who pays the piper, wins and Eastern wasn't about to contest her meaningful approach to the current problem.

"She's one stubborn bitch," he told himself in confidence. "Anybody else but her."

The following morning after breakfast, Joan found time to surprise even herself. It had become possible that acting on Eastern's slant with Dowling's new residency in mind had challenged her position.

"I've been thinking Mike…"

"Go on, I'm listening."

"It might be a good idea for me to get away for a few days, make a complete break of things, you know?"

"You've obviously given it some thought Joan, and yeah, you've certainly got my blessing on that." He asserted. "Anywhere special in mind?"

"Yes I have actually, I'm thinking along the lines of paying my mother and step father a visit. They live at Framfield. It's very rural and the solitude will give me a chance to get my head together." Eastern's face clouded over with curiousity before replying.

"Would I be right in thinking that…" faltering in anticipation, he let her continue where she'd left off.

"If this is anything to do with my step father, then the answer to your would be question is a resounding yes! When I think back, we've never really hit it off. In fact, I've never sat down and discussed my feelings with him on the matter. Besides which, he retired some years ago."

"Uhm, ever since I've known you, I could sense that you had a problem in that direction." Pausing suddenly, he voluntarily allowed his thoughts to go off on a tangent. "Incidentally, something had just occurred to me, there's no reason why I shouldn't pay Dowling's flat in the Dials another visit. Assuming of course it hasn't been let yet. I still get the feeling that I might have missed something. The fact that Terry Bryant is dead now means that I need to furnish some evidence to support my claim that he and Dowling were more than just good friends. The all important initials that came to light if you remember, aren't substantial enough on their own to make a case. I need to step up a gear."

An hour later, a solemn looking Eastern watched Joan drive off, and dallied until she had exited the village before making a move himself. In no time at all, he found himself conversing with the slow witted caretaker. The result of which could possibly ensure that his visit might be a fruitful one.

Apart from the fact that the flat itself had been legally vacated, and was due for re letting in 48 hours gave him carte blanche to search the premises at will. An additional bonus being that any original rubbish set aside for disposal still remained in situ. Eastern, it has to be said, was now on a high as he entered the flat. He was greeted by a sea of mounting rubbish, lying on a carpet of discarded mail and dated newspapers, and what looked like, at first glance, a plastic bag containing various personal effects.

One man's mess is another man's treasure, it seems. Or so Eastern would tell you. Almost immediately, he made the bag his own. "This is the closest I'm ever likely to get to 'Aladdin's Cave'. Dowling might just as well have left me a first edition of 'This is your life'. Up ending the bag, he allowed the contents to spill out on to the floor. Like a rat on heat, he delved amongst the rubbish, eyes darting everywhere. Stopping off briefly he queried a half hidden book of spent cheque stubs. "Geronimo!" he exclaimed and proceeded to examine every counterfoil in detail.

As hunches come and go, he now found himself on a higher buzz than an aggravated wasps nest. By means of deduction, it became apparent that there were three consecutive amounts of money spread over a 5-6 weekly period of time, reaching back some two months previous, and all listed toward one beneficiary, with the initials TB. Containing his 'find' became something else. "Gotcha!" he stormed, you're not the clever bastard that you thought you were Mr Dowling. You just made one hell of a clumsy mistake, and that is going to cost you dearly!"

His idea being, that cross checking the counterfoils against the original transactions would only be a formality only increased his partial conviction. The smug and contented face of a winner, said it all. "Johnnie Curtis will think it's his bleedin' birthday, once I've offloaded this little baby onto him." Any attempt to retrieve anything of any importance from then on, became superficial. Five minutes later and he'd seen enough. Handing the key back to the caretaker on leaving, Eastern reminded him to get back in touch, should his alleged 'brooms' show any sign of wearing out.

Before pulling away, he notified DS Curtis and arranged to meet in the car park at the Division in an hour's time. "It'll give me time for a cup of tea," he mused. The smile on his face later, looked like remaining permanent, prior to handing the evidence over. And Curtis was quick to show his appreciation.

"Good shot Mike…I guess this wipes our slate clean wouldn't you say? Forensic and myself are going to have a field day checking this exhibit out."

"Just call it a dress rehearsal mate, I'm on a roll at present." He quipped. "But do keep me up to speed…yeah?" Some time later, while relaxing in the confines of a cool bath, his nearby mobile kicked off. "Good I'm relieved that you got there all in one piece Joan…me? I'm soaking for want of a word…yeah…it's good news, I'll explain later…be in touch…bye."

For a second he appeared to be transient and locked in thought. "I think I'll give that pub around the corner a once over tonight. Yeah… I'll do that." He then settled back amidst a mountain of foam, and lost himself whilst wearing a classic look of contentment.

Chapter Ten
Your drink's on me!

It's often said that there are waterholes… 'spit and sawdust', and somewhere in this congested spirit world there are pubs. And Mike Eastern wasn't about to be disappointed in knowing that cosmopolitan Brighton had nothing to prove in that direction. Earlier on that evening he had come to the conclusion that a blend of Scotch, combined with 'Joe Public' as a chaser would amount to a good call in the Mermaid, a few minutes walk away from the square in Western Road. "It would give me the impetus I need to create a leveller." He told himself.

Nudging the door open to the side entrance, he adjusted his vision before making his way across the bar. Propping himself up on a stool he contented himself by gazing around the periphery of the bar itself. For the time of night he noted that business was relatively quiet. His observation then came under fire due to a young, rather ugly and pretentious looking barmaid who arrived on the scene ready to take his order, although, two drinks later, he would have been prepared to swear that she came across as Miss World. Then the illusion folded as the chewing gum that was playing catch up with her teeth, decided to surrender by landing on the bar top as she reached out for an empty glass.

At least his Scotch wasn't getting away, as it freely drained off his palate. Three doubles later though his vision appeared to be less comfortable. Maybe he wasn't the drinker he thought he was. He swiftly overruled that notion. "A 20 plus year love affair with the devil's brew must count for something," he concurred. He then realised that his vision had been invaded by the extreme décor, confronting him exuding out of four walls, and in his face, consistent with a seventies retro throwback of colour, depicting psychedelic mania.

"Whatever happened to Flock wallpaper?" was one conclusion he toyed with. It was just after 10pm and the bar at this stage was beginning to come alive. The in-house buzz deriving from revellers, party goers and regulars alike, now threatened to outdo the explicit beat of disco music, that formed the back drop to an electric atmosphere. Eastern was on the point of draining his glass having decided that the toilet would be a better option to escape the hubbub for five minutes. His lips were now on short time as his Scotch never made it that far. This was due to the pressure from an alien force brushing against his body and, in doing so, lifting his elbow off the Richter scale and spilling what Scotch remained in his glass on to the floor in the process. To say that he was somewhat put out as opposed to being highly needled would be the equivalent of 'Excuse me' leading up to 'Which door would you prefer to be thrown out of?" There and then he decided that diplomacy would be the best call.

The unknown perpetrator instantly became the first to acknowledge the altercation as Eastern offloaded his redundant glass and confronted him.

"I'm sorry about that...I had nowhere to go...so damn crowded, allow me to get you another drink." There was nothing tried and tested that could have prepared Eastern for what was about to follow as the two finally came face to face. Even the dismal lighting as an excuse wouldn't have swayed his judgement. In the time that it takes to express "I told you so" recognition had already sunk in. Momentarily, Eastern felt stifled, and powerless to react for a thousand reasons. This was no run of the mill punter he was dealing with. He was adamant that he was eye to eye and dealing with his own depraved nemesis, namely Andy Dowling.

The whole scenario had only taken seconds, although in real terms a couple of months in coming to fruition as a wheel of destiny now finally turned full circle. It might have been the thought of a possible

'Oscar' in the offing, or maybe he was just in shock but Eastern offered up his now defunct glass and mumbled, "That'll cost you a large Scotch I'm afraid."

Devoid of any emotion, Dowling produced a £5 note and handed it over saying "be my guest." Seconds later, he became history as a crowd of seasoned piss artists swallowed him up. So! To what depths would you go to when coming to terms with a situation like that?

In hindsight, Eastern could have walked away by accepting the loss of his Scotch and learnt nothing. Only here was a man who thinks on his feet in spite of the altercation. Without any hesitation he proceeded to pick the glass up from off the bar using a hanky and secured it in his pocket, alongside the £5 note. The look on his face at that point was priceless, as he muttered under his breath "Thanks for the drink you arsehole, and better still the DNA that goes with it." Turning on his heel he swiftly left the pub and headed steadfastly back towards the square.

Shortly after arriving back at Joan's apartment, he envisaged the thought that a long night lay in the offing. For the third time in less than five minutes he checked his watch. He was still on a high, alone and restless. He was also aware that what the night had to offer in terms of the Brighton scene had only just begun to kick in. It became clear that the effects surfacing from the Mermaid experience were still plainly visible. "Uhm...10.45pm" he grunted. But then he already knew that anyway. At least he had the genesis of a system in mind, by deciding to facilitate his emotions, and purge his mobile instead. Right now, it looked more tempting than his token nightcap. At the last moment, he decided to stall that idea as an irritant image of DS Curtis burst his bubble. "I guess it would be bad timing, even for Johnnie. Tomorrow's another day. It's not as if Dowling is going anywhere."

Early the next morning Eastern could be found submerged in a deep conversation with Joan, relating his inconceivable brush with Dowling. "As I say Joan, you couldn't have written the script. Surreal doesn't come into it, I got that close, I felt that I was underneath the guy's skin."

"Good God! The very thought makes me shudder. It's just as well that I opted for a break when I did." She replied thankfully. "The notion that I could have been present at the time…" She left off to regain her composure, and continued, although she was clearly shaken, "I'd rather we didn't talk about it, if you don't mind?" Eastern readily acknowledged her demand and attempted to reassure her.

"In a profitable way, I feel that the altercation was meant to be, stupid as that may seem. When you bear in mind what I managed to walk away with."

Prior to terminating their conversation, Joan mentioned the fact that her step father without prompting had let it be known that he had been making an in depth enquiry himself into the case. "Which I thought was rather strange at the time," she added.

48 hours after his altercation, the reaction from DS Curtis after Eastern had managed to pin him down, gained the type of response he'd hoped for. "Just to let you know Mike that the evidence you produced proved to be a windfall. Forensics have managed to resurrect a print from off the cheque stubs. Also, the glass itself had more going for it than a passport." Eastern then capped their conversation off with his own version of events by declaring, "A good result, onwards and upwards."

Chapter Eleven
A close encounter

In the event his enthusiasm towards the case although gathering momentum, climaxed suddenly, alluding from the side effects of a double edged sequel. "A smack in the mouth would have been a better result." Eastern confirmed later. Like the majority of the tabloids, the 'Clarion' hadn't missed a full stop.

'SUPERGRASS' MURDER SUSPECT IN U TURN
A late statement issued by the police has revealed that the security guard suspect held in the ongoing bung case has now accepted a clemency deal in lieu of new information. This information linked DCI Conway as part of a conspiracy to silence the crown prosecution witness, the whistleblower, aka DC Terry Bryant, who was recently found dead while living in a 'safe house' monitored 24/7 by the police. Conway, who is already on remand, while awaiting trial on further conspiracy charges, is the son of Sir Daniel Conway, the present assistant Police Constable. When approached for a statement by the press, the latter declined the offer for legal reasons. It has also been confirmed by a spokesperson for the IPCC that the fresh evidence could bring about a further arrest per se.

Looking decidedly grim, Eastern helped himself to another coffee, and glanced over the report once again, to satisfy himself that he hadn't missed anything. In return, his own slant on the case wasn't about to become wanting, and even less predictable as most others.

"One lousy rotten apple, that's all it takes, and bingo! All of a sudden you've inherited a fucking cartload." Shaking his head in frustration just came naturally to him. "Shit! You've got a lot to answer for Mr flaming Conway, your in it so deep you'll wind up doing your time in a bleedin' well."

Fifteen minutes later found him chilled out on the park bench adjacent to Dowling's flat. Fully engrossed with reading the 'Lambeth Serial Killer' he failed to spot a distinctive figure walking across the grass toward him. In no time at all, the man had now drawn abreast of him. Caught between being one page away from a fictional murder, and reality, the inviting question on offer became briefly lost in translation.

"Excuse me, haven't we met before somewhere?" The stranger enquired. Eastern didn't need the advantage of a retake to exact the sudden confrontation he now found himself facing. The earthy tone of the voice alone was drilling a hold inside of his head as recognition allowed a dormant instinct to kick in. Casually, and in a controlled manner, he slowly lowered the paper down before conversing.

"Sorry, you were saying?" In one brief split second, his intuition had proved to be on course. For the second time in 48 hours, he now found himself at odds, facing the haunting figure of Andy Dowling, no less.

"The Mermaid, wasn't it? The other night as I recall, I unfortunately spilt your drink. Once again you have my apology, I presume that you live in the village as well?" He went on. Eastern was propelled into thinking on his feet, he couldn't afford to come across as hostile.

"Yeah, you're right on the first count, but don't lose any sleep on it. But no, I happen to be here on holiday...which reminds me..." He broke off to check his watch. "God, is that the time? I'm sorry, I need to be somewhere else. Bye now." Dowling appeared to linger as Eastern hurriedly left, unaware that he was deliberately heading in the opposite direction to the flat. It was a necessary decision and well worth the walk around the block just to clear his head. He even managed a wry smile at one point, when considering the degree of familiarity that he had built up between himself and Dowling.

"It's almost got to the stage now whether or not I suggest to him your place or mine?" He would jokingly tell Joan, over the phone

A close encounter

that night. During their conversation Joan mentioned the fact that she would be leaving Framfield tomorrow morning arriving back at the flat around midday. A week had now lapsed since their ill timed confrontation in which time, in spite of stringent surveillance, Dowling appeared to have gone to ground, yet still he persisted. The last couple of hours had dragged on, and he was prepared to call it a day. He'd read the newspaper so many times the print had started to run. Just then his attention was averted to a taxi which had pulled up outside Dowling's flat. The driver alighted and disappeared inside the building. "He's obviously dealing with a call." Eastern remarked out of interest. Having had the best of the daylight, he decide to call it a day and head back to his apartment. The one consolation being "At least I'm assured that Joan will be back tomorrow." Moments later, any relief he'd procured became short lived by the sound of his mobile kicking in. Immediately, a look of consternation crossed his face as he glanced at the screen in recognition. "Johnnie! Hi mate, what's occurring you must be working on overtime?" The strained voice of Curtis's reply prepared Eastern for what was about to follow.

"I realise it's a bit late in the day Mike, but I must warn you that it's not good news I'm afraid. In a word, the IPCC in their wisdom have thrown out the Dowling case."

"On what grounds, for God's sake?" Eastern spluttered.

"Would you believe it, a lack of insufficient evidence?"

"Hell! That's knocked the shit out of me mate, I honestly envisaged the submission to be a walk in the bleedin' park."

"You and me both Mike. All the groundwork was in place, we had a match on the prints, and the bank statements tallied with the deposits that Dowling had made over to Bryant."

"Is it me, or have I missed something? It's just not adding up." Eastern fired back. It was clear that he was getting heated, leaving Curtis to opt for a compromise.

"Basically, they're saying that the Crown has to prove that the monies that had been exchanged had been procured for illegal reasons. And..."

"...And with Bryant lying in the morgue, we have got no poxy chance of proving a damn thing!"

"I'm sorry mate, but there it is. The situation is out of my hands, and I'm gutted. I would have bet good money knowing that Dowling would have been a certainty to go down."

Eastern then went on to explain his own theory, regarding their alleged relationship. "The way I see it, I reckon that Dowling contacted Bryant after leaving the force. And together they devised a compensation 'scam' based on the inside knowledge that Bryant had access to from his involvement with DCI Conway. I also think that apart from a percentage gain from the scam, Bryant wanted a 'sweetener' up front for the inside information he'd collected. Hence the three payments that came to light."

"Yeah, I can see how that makes sense, and your client, how does she fit in all of this?"

"That's the easy part. She would be Dowling's insurance, in the event that anything went wrong. So as I say, it was paramount on his part to 'groom' her should any unnecessary grief get in this way."

"You've got to hand it to him, he's one conniving operator. So I presume this all stems from when you initially contacted me, am I right?"

"Yeah, you got it. That's when Mrs Conway first came onto the scene."

"I presume we are talking about Joan Travers here?"

"Precisely the same. I reckon she had me shortlisted on the rate of one to zero as a shoulder to cry on, due to my previous with her estranged husband. And so apart from Bryant getting mullered, the rest you know anyway mate."

"When you think about it, the guy was so unlucky." Curtis concurred. If there was ever going to be a victim of circumstance it was him. There was nowhere for him to run, although he couldn't have known it at the time. But whatever the outcome, you have to say he was a two time loser."

"Absolutely! No question about it." Eastern added. "But saying that, I do have a problem with the word circumstance in this case."

"In retrospect, you and me both mate. What you've told me thus far isn't in the same ballpark in comparison. I realise I'm repeating myself but whoever was responsible for making the decision to eradicate

Bryant tells me that it had to come from a higher authority." Curtis declared.

"Fortunately mate, the IPCC don't give a shit about rank, they're only in for brownie points. You know as well as I do mate, one whisper, and they're over you like a bleedin' rash. I'd lay money that right now there's one or two twitching arseholes on the force as we speak." Their revealing and composite conversation came to a close minutes later with DS Curtis suggesting that they get together for a drink shortly.

Over a liquid supper that evening, Eastern found himself mind wrestling with an aspect of Dowling's alleged background, prior to his involvement in the case.

Supposition or otherwise, it certainly hadn't managed to manifest itself overnight. Eastern had held a nagging doubt for some time now, over the legitimacy concerning Dowling's claim that he indeed had terminal cancer. There and then, he decided to cover some old ground the following morning. And where better to start looking than back at Dowling's original address, adjacent to the 7 Dials?

"Blimey! You back ere again guv? I'm starting to see more of you than the bloody owner!" The caretaker exclaimed. At least he'd given Eastern a format to work with.

"Could be the guy's got an allergy to brooms, that's one good reason why." Eastern jested. "Mind if I come in? I won't keep you long. I'm hoping that you might unlock some answers I'm looking for." The man ushered him along the hall into a small living room, and indicated towards a chair, which Eastern readily declined.

"So, how can I help yer?" The caretaker enquired.

"If it's all the same with you, I'd like to talk about our mutual friend Mr Dowling. How long did you say you'd known him for?"

"Uhm, let's see now. I've been ere roughly eighteen months, so we're talking about eight or nine weeks I reckon…yeah that would be about right." Instinctively, Eastern felt his gut tighten in response to his own hidden agenda.

"Really, is that all? So why do I get the impression you've known him longer than that?" The caretaker, for reasons of his own, then elected to go on the defensive.

"Search me guv, you never asked me before, so I never said." Eastern nodded and smiled.

"Relax, you're right of course, I should have known better." Patronising? Maybe, but he couldn't afford to unnerve the man. There was too much riding on his hearsay.

The man then went on to say ,"The flat in question had become vacant and the landlord had advised him that a certain Mr Dowling would be taking possession over..." he shopped short. "Strange when I think back."

"Keep talking, I'm listening." Eastern urged.

"Well, why he never mentioned to me the length of his tenancy, which I thought unusual at the time. So when I questioned..." He stopped short before continuing. "I can quote him as saying, you do the job I pay you to do, and I'll do the rest. Just treat him like the other tenants. So now I'm thinking to myself, what's so bloody special about him anyway? And that's when he told me the business about him being terminal, plus his old man's involvement with the law."

"I assume by that, you mean your governor?" Eastern established.

"Absolutely!"

"He comes across as being an easy going sort of guy, your governor that is." The caretaker, Eastern noted, was suddenly looking decidedly uneasy, giving the impression that he wanted renege on his last statement.

"Well, not exactly on a personal level that is." He managed to blurt out. Eastern by now, was beginning to show signs of frustration.

"You've lost me for a minute sunshine. I thought that you said..." He wasn't given the chance, as the man intervened, by issuing a verbal roller coaster.

"I mean, that was the message he left with the agency who runs his business interests. He's got property all over, and lives abroad most of the time. In fact, I've never even met him on a personal level, know what I mean."

There and then Eastern came to the conclusion that he'd heard enough to convince himself that there was more to Andy Dowling than he'd been led to believe. He even started to question his own theory that the latter had been part of a complex scam. The gut feeling he'd had recently was now showing birth toward an alternative angle on the case overall. Especially when considering its intensity and the high stakes involved in knowing what certain individuals had to lose. If at any time he ever wanted a wake up call, it had to be now as his instincts called out for a steward's enquiry.

Dowling's existence from the time he'd taken the original flat and leading up to his present address had been erratic to say the least. Especially coming from somebody who's present status had been allegedly labelled as being terminal per se. "I just can't put my finger on where the guy is coming from anymore, his life is too bracketed for my liking. The fact that he's now cosied up in the village beggars belief. It's almost as if he knows more about my life than I do about his. While at the same time it could be that he's trying to tell me something. One thing is certain, he isn't your every day stereotypical career criminal, in spite of the evidence attached to him. And that is what really bothers me! As things stand, I'm battling away with Joan, Dowling and myself in one corner as being a separate identity, or so I'm led to believe. And in the opposite corner, festering away, you've got the bung case. In which, through unknown circumstances, could well involve just about everybody, whose earmarked as being in the bigger picture of things."

Up until now, Eastern had considered that his share of the dice, although serious in itself, had consisted of a 24/7 game, plus the added benefit of a well paid lifestyle that you only find in glossy magazines. At least, he had the firm satisfaction of knowing that Joan would be back from her recent trip of convenience that same day. In no time at all the illusion became shattered, thanks to his mobile, as he was about to gain entrance to his apartment. One hasty glance to confirm who the caller was did enough to satisfy himself that something untoward was in the offing.

"Hi Johnnie, how are you doing? You almost caught me on the hop. What can I do for you?"

The reply from DC Curtis, although well intended, came across as being double edged. "Right now Mike, I could use a one way ticket to fucking Brazil, and I mean it. The establishment, for want of a better word, are doing their utmost to seriously piss me off."

"Can you elaborate on that mate? It doesn't sound too healthy."

"No? Then get this. In a nutshell Mike, I'm off the case full stop, or until I've been told different."

"This has to be some sort of a bleedin' joke mate. How and why?"

Curtis went on to explain that he'd been given the cold shoulder treatment in his pursuit of damning evidence, notably, a DNA report released by the forensics. Eastern was still in disbelief mode and continued: "But surely, by pulling the plug on you, they've created a conflict of interest. And, more to the point, for what ever reason? No, I don't buy it. I'll be honest mate, it stinks. I mean, what ever happened to loyalty?"

Curtis also stated that the acting DCI who relieved Conway was under orders from upstairs to cocoon certain lines of investigation relevant to Dowling's role in the case. At that point, Eastern decided to confide his own latest thoughts to Curtis. And finished by stating: "That in my view, the only solitary factor coming out of this unholy mess, worth any credence at all now points to Dowling emerging as a leading player. What is it about this arsehole that makes him seem so bleedin' bullet proof? This happens to be the second time around he's had a let off. Firstly the CPS (Crown Prosecution Service), and now this latest revelation. If I didn't know any better Johnnie, that in spite of his actions in the case so far, it almost makes me wonder if the guy is a 'plant'. But that would be bollocks wouldn't it?" (At a later date, and with modified hindsight, he might be well subjected into eating those very same words.)

It was also noticeable that Curtis in reply, kept his own conclusions on the matter close to his heart. He curtailed their highly sensitive conversation by declaring: "You know as well as I do Mike, supposition and the truth might as well be a million miles apart. And moreover, who's the key person behind the scene pulling all the strings? If I didn't know any better, I'd have to say that your definition of a 'Mr Big' lurking in the background is looking more kosher by the minute."

Easing himself back into his armchair some time later, Eastern took full control of a large Scotch on the rocks. Deep in thought, he methodically rolled the glass backwards and forwards across his brow. Finally he raised it aloft before speaking in a subjective manner.

"Here's to you Mr Dowling, or whoever you are. I strongly advise you to make the most of the luck you've had on your plate so far. Just remember, I've got mine to come yet."

He'd barely downed his drink when Joan phoned to say that she was less than fifteen minutes away from him.

Chapter Twelve
An unprecedented date

It has often been stated on many occasions, that good company can prove to be expensive. Although, in Eastern's particular case, a fish orientated dinner washed down with a bottle of selected Chianti, proved to be a small price to pay for satisfaction. Especially when sharing the moment with a personal client, within the trappings of a renowned restaurant in the 'Lanes' in Central Brighton. An hour later, a much gratified Eastern gestured with his hand to indicate that he'd had enough and, at the same time, wiped his mouth with a serviette.

"So, how was that for you Joan?"

"Sorry!" For a second Joan looked slightly bemused.

"The sole!" He hastened to add. "Did it taste as good as it looked?" Her face then gave way to a knowing smile in favour of the genuine content to the question.

"If you're asking me was it worth waiting a week for, then I feel sure that you know the answer to that one Mike. And, by the way, it's lovely to be back in the village once again. Especially after a boring week in Framfield, so I'm really looking forward to all the latest gossip." From the moment that Joan had suggested that she felt the urge to eat out, Eastern responded by going on the defensive, strictly with the intention of leaving his work indoors.

"Sorry Joan, but I'd rather we take a rain check on any outstanding news. Besides, it's been a great evening, meaning that just for once, business isn't on the menu...okay?" For a brief moment, she appeared to remain aloof, before extending a silk-like hand to cover his which was resting on the table. She then smiled in her own exclusive manner. It was the sort of smile that made you think your heart had become a toboggan, speeding hell for leather on the great Cresta run.

"You can be such a klutz sometimes Mike." She responded. "But you're right of course." And slowly withdrew her hand but not before indicating that her glass was empty. Almost an hour later, 11.45pm to be precise, Eastern removed his bank card from off the service plate and requested the waiter to call for a cab.

"Thanks for a great evening Mike, and for what you didn't say." Joan expressed as she made the passenger seat in the cab her own.

"I'd almost forgotten the formula Joan." He exclaimed with sincerity. "But the rapport certainly worked. I'd like to think that it becomes a habit, yeah, the date was a good call."

"Where would you like to be dropped off sir?" Briefly lost in their own translation of the evening's events, the pair were interrupted by the driver seeking a drop off point.

"Sorry, make that Brunswick..." He faltered. "Tell you what, on second thoughts you can drop us off at the West pier, the walk will do us good...thanks." Still feeling high on a blend of good food, wine, and magnetic company, Eastern appeared to be oblivious to the fact that they were now heading in the complete opposite direction to where they intended to go. It was finally left to Joan to realise that something was amiss.

"You did say the West pier didn't you Mike?"

"Sure, why is there a problem?"

"Most definitely, I know Brighton well enough to know we are approaching Rock Gardens. That's the complete opposite direction."

Eastern had heard enough, and allowed his current mood to make a temporary diversion. Any frustration was lost on his fist, as he tapped the glass security panel. "Hey driver! What the bloody hell are you playing at?" He volleyed. "I didn't book a mystery tour." If the driver at any point had any inclination as to what was going on behind him, it didn't rub off on his body language as the cab lurched forwards, due to the sudden induction of speed. Within minutes of leaving behind the chilled environment of a quality restaurant, they now found themselves subjected to an unknown situation that they had no control over, while at the same time, held at the mercy of a mysterious manic driver, hell bent on a death wish, or so it seemed.

At this stage, any dialogue was rendered obsolete, as the pair were now forced to cling to each other, hoping to seek some form of security.

Rendered useless, the pair were thrown from side to side, as the vehicle ate up the corners of the back doubles that could be found in the bowels of the inner city. Eastern did what was possible to calm Joan down to a necessary degree of normality. The sheer force of terror inflicted on her had ripped her apart, causing her to sob hysterically. And then suddenly, the madness was aborted, as their roller coaster of hell at last came to a screeching halt. Visually Eastern could make out a large metal roller door that at first glance appeared to belong to an industrial type of building.

Acting on blind instinct, he immediately peered through the nearest window, in a vain attempt to see if he could make any connection as to the locale. The sparse street lighting did little to aid his cause. The gloomy night shadows only succeeded in mocking his futile attempt. Rapt in his own private war, Eastern was now unaware that the roller door had now been raised open, allowing the cab to enter. A sudden injection of blazing light directed from a torch beam, then hit him between the eyes, causing him to shield them.

In spite of this blinding handicap, his priority still lay with Joan, who could now be found cowering in the back seat, to all intents and purposes, suffering in an obvious state of complete and utter shock. He reached out to console her, and only succeeded in running into a wall of threatening demands. At this point any physical contact became non negotiable due to an alien voice invading his space. "Out! Now. Both of you, this is as far as you go."

Self preservation is one thing, but the bright glint issuing from the barrel of a .38 COBRA revolver or 'snubbie' fingered by the manic driver, swiftly extinguished any form of heroics from Eastern's mind. Besides which, his blitzed mind was now three laps behind any form of just reasoning, in respect of the scenario in which he'd been handed. Indeed, the small amount of brain he had been able to muster would have run to a no contest with sanity in mind.

"If this is hell..." he told himself. "Then I'm holding a valid ringside seat." In the background the distinct sound of the roller doors closing behind them now only promised himself and Joan an exclusive backdrop of undulating misery. Even their assailants were less than recognisable shadows, due to the extreme lack of light.

Without any prompting, the figure who was brandishing the torch, waylaid Eastern's thinking. "This lousy light is cracking me up, I reckon we're secure enough now don't you?" He enquired.

"I don't have a problem with that." The driver replied with an air of confidence. "The switch you're looking for is over in the corner, you can throw it now." Within seconds, the relief emitting from a dozen or so strip lights stuttered in a strobe like fashion, before reaching their potential. Eastern immediately threw his arms around Joan and drew her trembling body against his own. The pungent smell amounting from disused oil and petrol filled his nostrils as he cast his eyes around their surroundings. It quickly became apparent to him that they were now holed up in what resembled a run down garage workshop.

The driver meanwhile casually removed his hat and threw it to one side, as the pair looked up to confront their tormentors. A sustained hiatus of silence ensued as a transfusion of recognition slowly but surely absorbed their distorted minds. In sense, what was now on offer at first glance, contrasted with a remix of total horror and abhorrent fear coupled with the fact that as from now, they could well be acting out a grim dress rehearsal as a prelude to certain death and that they were the only two players in the cast.

Unfortunately for them, the director could be seen to be holding a revolver in lieu of a script, leaving his role to figure highly in the credits. Now came the time for Eastern to think on his feet, as a survival pattern kicked in. It was never going to be the greatest 'scene' he was ever going to play, indicating that he only needed the benefit of one take to get his view across. Considering his less than delicate situation, he still contrived to retain optimistic in a bid to gain a lifeline.

"Well...well, why aren't I surprised?" The clinging observation was aimed at the figure whom Eastern clearly thought could well be the mouthpiece of the two. "Although I can't speak for your...friend!"

Dragging out the implication, he nodded towards his assailant's accomplice. "But I have to tell you, that just lately, you're getting to be one fucking bad habit..." He stalled to emphasise his point, before ramming it home, "Mr Dowling."

A cryptic smile, that could have suggested war or peace either way crossed his aggressor's face, before the gunman replied in a melodramatic manner.

"I'll take that as a subtle observation, but you're right of course, Mr Eastern." Hesitating briefly, he caressed the revolver against his cheek, and continued in the same vein. "Unfortunately, like most traits, habits have a tendency to die from time to time, if you'll excuse the pun? So I feel sure that you and Mrs Conway, or should I say, Travers, both have a shared interest in living?" Meanwhile Dowling's henchman began showing signs of restlessness, as he cut in.

"Forget the verbal bollocks Dowling, let's just do what we came ere for. The sooner I'm out of ere the better I'll like it!" His ranting outburst as intended, made little or no impact to the situation, simply allowing Dowling to pursue his one man persecution. For her part, Joan was now on the verge of breaking up completely, leaving Eastern struggling to support her.

As clichés go, it was never going to be the best on offer when facing apparent death, and Dowling made it his own. "It seems such a shame, and I apologise to you both, just when we were getting to know each other as well." In the background his sidekick was almost screaming at him now, to cut short the charade.

"Do it! Fucking well do it! You idiot...let's get the hell out of ere." Slowly and deliberately Dowling cocked the weapon, and extended his firing arm at shoulder height, ensuring that Eastern would be his first nominated victim. A highly noticeable and discerning look then masked his face as he prepared to pull the trigger. Eastern literally froze as he looked down the barrel of the .38. He wanted to speak so badly, to say anything, but he couldn't. Even his heart had gone walkabout, and his dislodged brain could be found in his mouth, permanently choking him.

"Think man! No time...action!" Again, useless...arms, legs numb. His bloodless knuckles were now showing white from tension as he braced his body for the inevitable coupe de grace. Dowling's finger, slowly tightened around the trigger. For Eastern, it would be the last visual memory in time afforded to him. What developed next became inexplicable. In less time than it takes to breathe in there followed a muffled explosion as Dowling in a rehearsed and business like manner suddenly spun around and fired point blank at his side kick. The impact from the bullet rocked the man's body back on his feet, giving the appearance of an oversized macabre puppet. Instantaneously, to the right of his temple, a 10mm neat blackened hole gave way to a forced trickle of blood. The look of horror and utter amazement featured in his death mask became apparent the moment Dowling pulled the trigger. With nothing to sustain him anymore, the victim's lifeless body slumped to the floor resembling a useless heap of flesh and bone. As if counting by numbers, Dowling then proceeded to walk across to the victim's lifeless form. On reaching down, he felt for a token pulse with his free hand. Any lip reader of substance would have had a field day standing 20 yards away as Dowling spoke in a nonchalant manner. "Uhm, just as I anticipated, dead before he hit the ground."

Content to continue in the same implausible vein, he then turned his attention back towards the mesmerised forms of Eastern and Joan. But not before disarming, and secreting the weapon inside his jacket. Anything that the two had wanted or might have attempted to say became lost in translation as Dowling opened up once more.

"I apologise to you both once again, for having to witness that spontaneous scenario. But I can assure you, it was absolutely imperative. As from now, you will need to trust me and my actions, therefore I suggest that you get back in to the car and try to relax. In the meantime, I have a few loose ends I need to deal with." Impervious to any criticism that he'd rewritten a designer script, in a matter of seconds Dowling motioned the pair over to the car. Satisfied that they were out of earshot, he made an arranged call from his mobile.

The orders were rubber stamped and Eastern wasn't about to argue. Finally, he was verging on the good side of normality. "Life is for living, for fucksake!" He fully convinced himself. Without further hesitation he swept a delirious Joan Travers up into his arms, a minute later they were huddled together in the cark, seeking a form of solace.

Seemingly locked in conversation, Dowling could be seen pacing up and down, watched over by a tentative and much relieved Eastern. Or so he had thought.

To all intents and purposes, his current position had suddenly morphed into another nightmare. He could only look on in utter dismay as Dowling pocketed his phone in exchange for the revolver, which he methodically rearmed before approaching the car. Eastern did his best to shield Joan, anticipating the worst was to follow. "The poor bitch won't know what's hit her," he told himself despairingly. At the last moment, Dowling stopped short, as he drew abreast of his alleged accomplice's dead body. Consistently wiping the gun clean, he placed it into the palm of the victim's hand, before confronting Eastern once more. Under the circumstances, the latter decided to let Dowling do the talking. His opening gambit was bizarre to say the least.

"Probably like yourself, I like to keep things nice and tidy, you know how it is." In an instant, the moment became surreal, as a vision of his bed sit entered his subconscious. The scene caused him to laugh involuntarily, knowing that Dowling had murdered someone in cold blood just moments before. Dowling's take on the situation far outbid his own thoughts, by adding another name to 'tidy'. And then the situation as a whole melted into history as Dowling continued. "Just for the record, I have some additional transport arriving shortly, and we…" he circulated with his hand and continued, "We need to make another journey. I would ask that you be patient at this time. That is, until it's possible to fully explain my actions."

For his part, Eastern was having a problem coming to terms with Dowling's sublime approach to the position now surrounding the three of them. Putting his own trauma to one side briefly, he recalled himself attempting to analyse the depth of the latter's mind, at a previous moment in time. The stronger he contested it, the clearer it became, that his version of the man's integrity hadn't been swayed, in spite of this latest soul destroying experience. For the moment, the facts of the matter were put on hold, as a small adjacent service door suddenly opened. Eastern watched intently as a figure in dark garb and matching glasses entered. Having acknowledged the stranger, Dowling beckoned Eastern to follow him, along with Joan. Within seconds, the pair were blindfolded leaving Dowling to extinguish the lights in the lock up. Feeling powerless once again, they were ushered outside and put into a waiting car. Moments later the vehicle slid silently away from the kerb, engulfed in the prevailing mist, and swirling shadows of the night. The next voice they heard belonged to Dowling coming through the intercom system. "Please accept my apologies once again for the inconvenience of the blindfolds. They are merely a security precaution so I advise you not to tamper with them."

Having been forced to witness Dowling's murderous mood swings earlier on, the pair were resigned to just sit back and collect their addled thoughts. "Where do you think they're taking us Mike?" Joan whispered at length. "I don't know how much more of this I can stand." Eastern found her hand and gently squeezed it lovingly.

"Try and hang in there Joan, something tells me that we've had the worst of it." Adding, "It wouldn't surprise me if the bloody car is bugged, and who the hell is the other guy that's now involved?" The fact that they were subjected to dealing with complete darkness had jointly left their senses totally disorientated, thus rendering time and direction to become irrelevant. Mental exhaustion had now set in, and within minutes they were both mercifully sound asleep. Right now Eastern's subconscious could be found sitting on a dozen fences divided by as many dark conclusions, chiefly being were the past events considered to be an aspect of reality, or had it all been a sick illusion? Or maybe, it was one poxy dream that he'd inherited. If that was the case, then it was still ongoing, featuring a demanding alien voice attempting to infiltrate his space.

"Eastern! Wake up man, we have arrived at our destination and I need you to be on the case." And then it was all over. He couldn't be sure, but he guessed that it was Dowling in his face, shaking him, while at the same time giving orders to his companion. "I'll leave you to deal with Mrs Conway, you've got a couple of minutes and then we go."

"Whatever." Eastern told himself. "We've come this far...what the hell!" Doors...steps...corridors...ramps followed but not necessarily in that order and then dramatically came to a close at last. They were then ordered to remove their blindfolds. Truth to say, it was one order that they didn't have a problem with. Squinting and rubbing their sore eyes, they slowly adjusted to the profound light. Instinctively, Eastern looked around to search out his captors.

As it turned out, his aim became irrelevant, due to Dowling's impatience to open up a dialogue. "Please sit down and make yourself comfortable, and then hopefully we can discuss your position when the matter becomes clearer. Incidentally, I'm sure you could both use some refreshment after your ordeal, tea or coffee perhaps?" Under the circumstances, a mediocre glass of water would have tasted like champagne. Without any ado, Eastern ordered two coffees. A brief lull existed, giving Eastern the opportunity to take in his surroundings. He noted that the medium sized room was sparse to say the least, consisting of a couple of chairs, and a token table at best. Access was limited to one main door, and the décor itself was Spartan. Visions of an interrogation room remained central to his thinking.

Having succumbed to his coffee, and Joan's needs, Eastern found himself desperate for answers. As usual, his 'maverick' persona got the better of him, along with sarcasm as a companion. "I can't say that it's been a pleasure Mr Dowling, although I…" A raised hand from Dowling immediately checked him in full flight.

"We need to start the way that we intend to go on Mr Eastern, and it all starts here. I can categorically state here and now, that I was never at any time your Mr Dowling. 'Winner?' yes! For reasons that will become clearer later. As from now, you will only address me as Rogon. And I suggest, no, insist, that you take what I imply on board. Suffice to say, your life including Mrs Conway's could depend on it, do I make myself clear?" The genesis of his statement now evolved into another added bolt from out of the blue.

Eastern was losing it fast, he now found himself handling a ticking bomb, and he disposal formula could be found wedged in his mouth. Pointing at his coffee, the expression mounted on his face and relayed his sunken thoughts. Rogon hastily dismissed the gesture, and simply shook his head. "You have had a lot to deal with in a small amount of time Mr Eastern, so I can appreciate your scepticism….here." Picking up the offending cup, he downed the remaining coffee. "Um, not bad, even for Government issue." He ventured, and made a bad job of smiling in the process.

At least the ice was now broken, giving Eastern a verbal franchise on the situation. "You specifically mentioned the word Government Rogon, could you define your logic? Only from where I'm sitting, I'm having a problem dealing with it!"

From then on, Rogon exposed his plastic attitude, in keeping with his role. "Yes, let's move on from that. As things stand, yourself and Mrs Conway are being held here in a Government facility. Not, I hasten to add, for too long."

"No shit!" Eastern exclaimed. "How could I be that dumb?" He turned to Joan and nodded. "These guys are obviously security agents, I think we can at least relax at last."

"Indeed you can." Rogon concurred. "Although I much prefer the heading of 'spooks'." He stressed. Eastern's mind was now wide open, and he wanted more.

"Tell me, am I right in thinking that this whole bloody charade was for mine and Mrs Conway's benefit?" Rogon smiled in a cryptic manner, before replying in a conclusive manner.

"Your nobody's fool Mr Eastern, and I have to say, you have managed to keep the agency busy, since your intervention. And you Mrs Conway, could have done a lot worse, with regard to your own input. You must have realised by now that we had to set you both up, basically on the off chance that you might secure vital information, over and above our own, into bringing the existing conspiracy case to a close."

"Good God! And then there's the letters and the calls." Joan implored.

"Utter crap!" Care of yours truly, or 'winner' as I was referred to. They were all part of the game, besides which, you were both under 24/7 observation from day one. And I congratulate you Mr Eastern, on your findings and intuition. Oh, by the way, I think you may have previously met a colleague of mine?" Clicking his fingers became the signal to allow a figure dressed in black and wearing shaded glasses to enter the room. In his own time, he removed some wadding seated inside of his mouth, followed by his glasses and, in doing so, revealed the unforgettable and susceptible caretaker.

Eastern found himself momentarily stunned into silence by the transformation. "And there was me thinking, what an idiot." He spluttered.

"I had to let you think that." The man replied. "But do me a favour, don't you mention the word 'broom' to me again! Incidentally, it didn't take you long to find the all important cheque stub that I planted in the flat. And, before I forget, the lovely 'Rita' sends her love."

"Who the hell is Rita?" Joan demanded, glaring at Eastern.

"It's a long story Joan, we'll deal with that one later. Right now, I need to know where we both stand, now that I'm beginning to get a handle on the situation."

"I'm pleased that you've considered your options Mike, if you're happy for me to call you that?"

"Why not indeed?"

"I ask, simply because your work thus far hasn't finished just yet. We, and that includes yourself, should you accept the mission, need to expose the 'big one'. I feel confident that you can aid us to do just that. We are looking for an 'inside man', someone who's familiar with the way the system works. You're nobody's fool Mike, and we are well aware that you have an ongoing source and contact on tap."

"Says who?"

"Let's just say that I've known for some time Mike. By the way, how is DS Curtis? He comes across as being one of your own, wouldn't you say Mike?" Eastern shrugged his shoulders to symbolise defeat.

"I'm not even going to ask you what you might know about our relationship, but yeah, you're right as far as he's concerned."

"Wise man Mike, I even know the colour of your underpants!"

"Dismissing the personal attributes for a minute, surely you've got your own method of dealing with high level criminal activity?"

Rogon was emphatic when replying. "Of course we have without question…" He stopped short. "Or rather we did, until we unfortunately lost our whistleblower." Eastern's mouth dropped in utter disbelief at Rogon's disclosure.

"Are you saying that…"

"Yes!" he interrupted vehemently. "Our agent was a Government 'plant', the whole thing was set up to include the tabloids on our

An unprecedented date

behalf. That is how big an operation this is."

"And the arsehole who got 'blown' away shortly afterwards, where the hell does he figure in all of this?"

Rogon was resigned into holding his head, before seeking an answer. "I won't kid to you Mike, I'm afraid you're going to have to trust me on this one." He went on to explain that he himself had secured an inroad into the hired gang responsible for murdering the whistleblower. "As a result, I was seconded into acting as a paid 'hit man' to murder yourself and Mrs Conway, the climax of that resulting in the showdown earlier on tonight."

"But the firm wouldn't have known about my involvement right?"

"On the contrary Mike, it seems that a bogus phone tap happened to pick up on a certain conversation that you had with DS Curtis. The rest you can work out for yourself." Once again Eastern found himself wanting, eventually deciding to end on a lighter note.

"The Mermaid, the first time that we 'accidentally' met, if you recall? I never did get around to having that blasted drink. So I'll settle for another coffee if you don't mind, my eyes are telling me something. In the meantime, where do you propose that we go to from here?"

"Glad that you asked me that one Mike, so let me run this suggestion past you." Rogon went on to explain that Eastern would be inaugurated as a member of the acting IPCC team. His undercover role would entail investigating the records and files department at Central and HQ, hopefully to seek out any discrepancies. Any form of liaison regarding explicit information would come via a selected call box, manned by agent 'B' to save time and the letter itself would alternate on a regular basis to uphold security.

"And Curtis, what part will he play as from now?" Eastern demanded. It was almost as if Rogon had anticipated his question.

"As from yesterday, Curtis has been given grounds to take compassionate leave." A plastic smile clouded his face before replying, "I have it on good authority that his Grandmother is seriously ill."

"Christ sake! Rogon." Eastern exploded. "You people really are something else, do you know that?" Shrugging his shoulders, Rogon insisted on having the last word.

"We do what we do Mike, in spite of the fact it's seemingly uncivilised. But nevertheless it becomes a necessity should the situation be called into play. Who knows, one day you might get used to the system?" Ten minutes later and aptly blindfolded for security, the pair were placed in a car and driven back to the village, and not before Eastern had been instructed that at 3.30pm (it was now 2.45am) a car would arrive at the flat in Brunswick Square and transport him to spooks HQ for an induction period, followed by a general briefing.

Part of the deal made by Eastern included at 24/7 surveillance watch on the flat, knowing that Joan could still be vulnerable. It goes without saying that any outstanding sleep left to the pair early that morning, was duly accounted for, once they had been officially dropped off.

Chapter Thirteen
Under cover and underestimated

It was tedious, it was time consuming, it was Eastern's third day on the job, and it was damn uncivilised! "Bloody Rogon got it right, another hour of this and I'll be glad when I've had enough." Having decided that Central might be a good springboard to commence investigating the bung probe case, Eastern was now having strong reservations about his poached affiliation to the hallowed halls of Law and Order, including the inconsistency arising from the files that he was searching through. Stopping off briefly, he checked for an update on his watch. "God! Is that the time? I should have called Joan over an hour ago. She's not going to be very impressed."

He was almost on the verge of calling it a day, when his suspicions were aroused by one file in particular. Or, as he explained to 'B' later on in the day, "The lack of the contents that were listed." From what he could gather, without delving too deeply, it amounted to the loss of one independent and two other statements both of which were allegedly made while under caution. Although it has to be said, that the name on the file itself was never in dispute, and found to be classified as such. Namely, the 'Crown versus Henry Dowling'.

Over a belated dinner that evening, Eastern felt the need to digress over the day's events. This in turn, prompted Joan to do likewise. "No, you first Mike," she suggested. "I'm still struggling to come to terms with Dowling's admission that…"

"I presume of course that you mean Rogon, darling? There's a mountain of difference in knowing that Henry Dowling himself did actually exist. In fact the details arising from his case triggered this whole operation, from day one. As for the alleged Andy Dowling, he always was, and still remains a Government agency spook, AKA Rogon. We must never lose sight of that fact. It'll be hard, because I can see that it bothers you."

"And you Mike, what's your stand on what has transpired? You can't tell me that you haven't had reservations concerning your position? I sincerely hope that you understand who, and what, you're dealing with?" Toying with his Scotch wasn't the response that she was looking for.

Easing off on his glass, a double edged smile creased his face as he looked up. "I'm flattered that you have my best interests at heart Joan. You do realise of course that if I pursue this Government job, then you will no longer require my services. The only issue remaining that we will have left in common, is one of security. And Rogon is dealing with that aspect, as we speak."

The look that transformed her face began to have a two-sided effect. A simple 'yes or no' would appear to be a prelude too far. Deep down, she knew that she wanted more out of their relationship. The mere thought of total closure wasn't in her script. "Why can't we just leave things the way they are Mike? And pretend that this whole rotten mess never existed?" She pleaded. "Besides, I've got used to you being around."

It was the longest he'd ever taken to pour himself a Scotch, as his mind went off at a tangent. Delving into a track record that was littered with matrimonial disasters. "I must be a sucker for punishment," he told himself. "Although Joan is a classy bitch, in an exclusive way." But that's the crux of the matter stupid. It's because they are what they are that you've landed yourself with this problem. His subconscious was having a field day, and the jury was out.

"Mike!"

"Oh, sorry Joan, I was bloody miles away. Yeah, no, I mean that's fine. I'll stick around if that's okay with you?" On the odd occasion it sometimes pays to swim with the tide, and Eastern wasn't about to argue the case as the fullness of perfect sensuous lips suddenly locked onto his own. Somehow, the importance of his Scotch seemed to have lost its appeal. Suffice to say that when he did finally get round to drinking it, the quality appeared to have increased its maturity.

Early the following morning, the 'Clarion' issued them with an unexpected wake up call.

BUNG CASE BROUGHT FORWARD
After three preliminary hearings, it has been announced that the defendant DCI Conway will now appear at Lewes Assizes on Monday 14 August to stand trial on conspiracy charges.

Eastern looked up from the paper before echoing his own thoughts. "At least it's a start Joan. And even more interestingly will be to see what price loyalty will surface out of it. I am of course referring to family. Will you be attending the trial by the way? It's not as if you're a witness." She shook her head vigorously to pre-empt any likelihood of it every happening.

"Absolutely no way. Unless of course I was subpoenaed to attend in which case I would have to. No, I'll rely on you Mike, you can keep me abreast of the proceedings." It wasn't so much what he said, as opposed to the way that he said it, as Eastern explained.

"I'm afraid it will have to be the limited version from now on, under the circumstances."

"You mean..."

"Yeah" he interrupted, and laughed. "You do realise that I'm Government property now." For a spontaneous effort it became a close run thing, and Eastern did well to avoid the slice of toast she threw at him in fun. As prearranged, he made a covert call to 'B' that same day to update him with his findings regarding his stint at Central. His report was documented, and he was then advised to move on to Division.

Putting it mildly, and if asked, he wouldn't hesitate to be honest by stating "I've had a shit day at the office!" So when Eastern received a random call on his mobile, emerging from a likely source. The end result became the welcome shot in the arm he could never have envisaged.

"Hello, Mike Eastern speaking, how can I help?" In return, the reply he swiftly noted stank of 'old school breeding', which included a distinctive ring of worldly charm about it.

"Ah! I'm glad we have had this chance to converse at last old chap. By the way the name is Travers. Major Travers that is…retired of course." Eastern went from confusion one minute to total disbelief the next as the name slowly registered. It seemed like an eternity stranded in no man's land. "Hello, I say, are you still there dear boy?" The caller enquired.

Eastern finally gathered himself together, cursing inwardly at his stupidity. "Damn it! I should have known better." Although, in his defence, it's not every day that one gets a call from an ex Chief Constable.

"My apologies Sir, my phone hasn't stopped ringing over the last couple of hours," was the best excuse he could come up with at the time. In retrospect, his oversight didn't amount to a problem, leaving the Major to verify his cause.

"It isn't a bad thing to be in demand old chap, and that is the reason why I am phoning you." In his mind Eastern was having negative thoughts by allowing his past track record into his thoughts. "Shit! I can't wait for the verbal crucifixion that's coming," ran through his mind.

"I can assure you…"

"Relax old chap, you're in good company." Travers intervened and went on, "It's perfectly clear to me that we are on the same side here, and I'm a damn good 'bat' when I'm called upon…what!" he expounded.

"Yes sir, no Sir, three fucking bags full Sir!" was what Mike wanted to say. But he admired the Major's charisma all the same. "So, how can I be of service to you."

"Without being presumptuous Mike, if I can be so bold? I have a feeling that I'm in a position to help you, from what Joan has related to me. And I have to say at this juncture, that she comes across as being most contented, more than she has for a long time. All thanks to you my dear boy. This bloody awful business that you're both surrounded by, could use an injection of influence, what!"

Eastern wasn't about to argue, "I couldn't agree more, it's all about who you know Sir, as opposed to what you know, when push comes to shove. What did you have in mind, Major?"

"Well I won't dwell on any opinions for a start, as I feel sure that we both share the same conclusions. So now, I'm thinking in terms of knowledgeable back up, should a problem arise."

"My thoughts entirely Sir, money can't buy that aspect."

"Precisely, old chap. So I suggest that you contact a trusted ex colleague of mine, stationed at HQ, CS (Chief Superintendent) Gleason. Damn good chap to be around, what! I'll be following your progress at a distance, and good luck old man!"

He then rang off, leaving Eastern to ponder over a couple of beneficial issues he didn't have before. Just then, Joan entered the room as he was down loading his mobile. On looking up, he noticed that she appeared to be a trifle sheepish. "I presume by your manner, that you heard the conversation. It was your step father wanting to get in touch." He remarked casually.

"Oh really?"

Eastern was forced to grin. "Don't look so surprised, I'm sure that you knew he would at some stage?" Her face broadened into one of false recognition.

"Well he did mention the fact, last time we spoke. So, did anything come of it?" It became a throwaway line and she bowed to his supremacy.

"Yes! Fortunately, he's done me a great favour, and 'marked my card' in the process."

Full of apprehension, Eastern made himself known to the desk Sgt at Division the next morning. Who, in turn put him in touch with the IPCC team. Following a short preliminary discussion he was left to his own devices, sifting through unlimited files and dossiers dating back some six years previous.

Not withstanding the relevant files held and processed by the then prosecution as evidence, there was always the slim chance that something amiss could have been overlooked. One vital lead above all others would mean locating a specific signature, or reference on a contentious file that could be traced back to source and redefined. The said name itself, or authorisation stamp, was believed to hold the key if proven in bringing down 'Mr Big', the absolute brains behind the conspiracy.

It soon became clear to him in time, as he progressed, that in many selective cases, leading evidence submitted by the defence at that time appeared to have been held back, on alleged discretionary grounds. Bearing in mind the supreme importance of this disclosure, he found himself struggling to keep his thoughts to himself. "No bloody wonder they grounded Johnnie Curtis, he could see what was going down. God knows how many innocent people have been fitted up in lieu of an offshore investment."

Mulling over a midday coffee in the canteen, Eastern poured over the reference notes that he'd procured earlier on. One insignia in particular that he'd managed to glean earlier on appeared to be troubling him. "Uhm! SDC, the initials are just not working for me, in fact the letter S is really bugging me." It wasn't until he'd finished his second coffee, that a session of lateral thinking suitably put his reasoning back in the frame. "You bloody idiot Eastern!" he chided himself, "How could you be that dumb? The answer has been staring at you all along and you couldn't see it! The S doesn't have to represent a name, but moreover the leading part of a title instead." Finally it all fell into place as he adjusted his brain. "Sir Daniel Conway, assistant Police Constable, no less." He blurted out. "Hell, Rogon will have a field day on the strength of that."

Eastern was now fired up, allowing his brain to run wild on an injection of scenarios, including the omission of a well worn adage that hammered away inside. "Like father, like son." In the past, the mere possibility that the two Conways could somehow be linked in the conspiracy would only have run to conjecture on his part. Still out on a high, he milked the moment as he targeted his principal thoughts. "I strongly suggest that you two arseholes make the most of your borrowed time, your road to perdition is nearing a dead end."

As an off the cuff remark goes, only fate itself would be in position to clarify its two way legitimacy, although reality ends here. In so far as he was concerned, his day had been fruitful. Left with time on his hands, he made a snap decision to drop in on Gleason over at HQ, giving himself the opportunity to make himself known.

An hour later, on exiting a side door at HQ, he noted that the car park was almost full to capacity, leaving him with a slight problem in pin pointing the location of his car. As it turned out, he remembered leaving it close to the main exit for convenience sake. This in turn, was served by a one way system throughout.

With bearings now intact, he casually proceeded in the direction of his car. Glancing over his shoulder, he reminded himself to be aware of exiting vehicles approaching him from behind. One minute nothing, then suddenly a vision of hell on four wheels consumed his being. To be wise after the event is one thing, staying alive became paramount. The estimated speed of the vehicle rapidly bearing down on him left Eastern in no doubt that the intention behind the premeditated altercation was for his benefit. Question! How does one define a split second, in terms of thinking? For Eastern, it wasn't even an option, as the wheel screeching ominous vehicle reached its potential, hell bent on delivering a lethal package of designer metal neatly wrapped in a contrived death sequence of events. From that moment on, any form of reflex on his part materialised from a combination arising from ultimate shock and instant fear, amid the acrid stench exuding from burning tyre rubber and metal heat that now bore down on his body.

With all options barred, the nearest car bonnet proved to be his one remaining salvation as instinct kicked in. Every muscle, and every sinew in his frozen body combined in a last do or die attempt to avoid being mercilessly run down. Instinctively he hurled his frame sideways in the forlorn hope that he'd succeeded in his last ditch effort. The whole episode in its entirety had taken only seconds but to Eastern, it became sufficient enough to view a double take on his life. Then, just as swiftly as it had started, his nightmare was redundant, leaving his bedraggled body to slide unceremoniously off the car bonnet, and land in an un-majestic heap on the asphalt surface of the road.

Almost immediately, the sudden realisation of what might have been gripped his ravaged body, and in doing so, forced him to retch unashamedly. He found himself sweating profusely, in spite of a cold wave of alien air that consumed his body, causing his frame to involuntarily shake, and then tremble. Only this time it was in sheer anger and frustration, in knowing that he'd been deliberately targeted. Accepting the fact that the premeditated incident had been executed and where the danger itself had been conceived, was within the HQ precinct only aggravated the problem.

On considering the facts, to rush headlong into a private war with the same organisation he was trying to bring down wouldn't make any sense at all at this stage. At best he could use the experience, albeit a threat, as part of a learning curve in the art of security. Satisfying himself that the altercation had been a huge wake up call in more ways than one, now emphasised the danger that existed on a personal level. The irony was that the person, or persons, responsible for this latest charade to have him removed from the equation, could well be somebody already known to him. If this was the case, then his maverick style position could be even more vulnerable than previously. The time had now come to readdress his flagging existence. Rising shakily to his feet, he dusted himself off and, minutes later, climbed behind the wheel of his car. For the moment, he was content to sit it out, and regain some of his lost composure before driving off, although his overworked brain had other ideas by allowing his immune system to kick start a verbal defence.

"God almighty! That was a close call; I reckon I got lucky this time. It's clear that some nasty bastard wants me out of the way full stop! It can only be for what I know, I'm convinced of that." Without any prompting he found himself quietly laughing to himself as his mind took a u-turn by switching to a more positive streak. His actions became the shot in the arm that he craved as he voiced his own script. "Well I've got news for you, whoever you are, you've only succeeded in pissing me off some more. So, bring it on arsehole!"

His outburst became the edge he was looking for, "Just remember this, what I've got on you is now 'banged' up in here and awaiting a release date, that's something you can't take away from me baby." Slowly and methodically he tapped the side of his head. Seconds later, and still chuckling, he turned the key in the ignition and manoeuvred the exit. Twenty or so minutes later found him parked up in the village and, would you believe it, still smiling.

Sighing thankfully, Eastern reached out and grasped the inviting glass from her hand. "Thanks Joan, I'd almost forgotten what it tasted like." Forced to agree, Joan nodded decisively before hitting back to silence his statement.

"After taking in what has happened, I can only think that you're fortunate enough to have an opinion at all! This isn't a one off Mike, and you know it. These people are playing for high stakes, and using you as a pawn in the process. And as for those so-called spooks, hell! You don't owe them a damn thing."

Content to fall back on his Scotch as a cover, Eastern declined to reply, knowing that as an outsider looking in, Joan had inadvertently stated the obvious. Nevertheless, downing what remained in the glass stirred him into levelling Joan's own genuine observations. "It seems light years away since you initially decided to contact me. Like it or not Joan, I'm embroiled in this case right up to my neck, starting from day one, purely through fated circumstances Not that I'm complaining, but you need to know that nobody is pulling my strings. And, what's more, I don't envisage walking away from unfinished business. That isn't what Mike Eastern is about. The important thing to remember Joan is that we started this venture together, so trust me when I say that we will undoubtedly finish it together."

Chapter Fourteen
A level of understanding

Day one for the opening of the conspiracy trial affecting the accused, DCI Conway, and two further accomplices was now only three days away. Already the hype surrounding the case was beginning to make its mark at disparate degrees. For Joan in particular, the hiatus leading up to the trial and beyond would become one of personal retribution, the effect of which, if not handled with restraint, could evolve into a further trial of unprecedented grief. The tension now existing in their apartment had become somewhat flared from two directions. For his part, while acting on Rogon's orders via a briefing, Eastern had been ordered to step down until further notice – the unsuccessful attempt on his life being a major factor in making his decision.

Eastern, on the other hand, had ideas of his own, which didn't include carpet slippers and waiting for the phone to ring. "This isn't me Joan, I need to be out on the street getting busy, and embracing what I'm good at. Spooks I don't need! You said it yourself remember? Besides the outcome has become personal. That bastard who almost wasted me over at Division was obviously under orders, and probably a freelance face. Rest assured, somebody out there knows something that I don't. So I intend to dig around and see what I can come up with."

At first glance it looked like any other leather-cladded pocket note book. But the similarity as to its contents ended there. The book in question was Eastern's 'bible', and the priceless 'street' information

A level of understanding

it contained could well have graced the underworld hall of fame. Flipping through the pages he lost no time in winkling out two specific contact numbers. "Let's see, who's it going to be, Mickey Sexton or Ray 'news' Carter. Yeah, I reckon Sexton gets my nod assuming, of course, that he's not banged up again."

Dialling the number he required unfortunately didn't meet with the response he'd anticipated. "Hello darling, Trixie speaking. I'm with a client at the moment if you'd like to..." Eastern slammed the receiver down in frustration before she could finish.

"Yeah, yeah, I get the picture sweetheart, where is it this time Sexton, Belmarsh or the Scrubs?" he expressed in anger. Shaking his head, he quipped, "At least you're getting the bloody rent paid!" Without further ado, he moved on to the next number. "Right then! Let's see what you can come up with Mr flaming Carter. Hello...yeah, is that Carter?"

"Who the bleedin' hell wants to know?" Came back the curt reply.

"This is Mike Eastern speaking, you moron, and don't even think about hanging up, unless you've got friends abroad."

"Mr Eastern, would I fuck with you? I've got overheads too you know."

"Spare me the verbal diarrhoea Carter. You'd sell your own grandmother's wheelchair for a packet of cigarettes. Now, listen up. I'm after some gilded SP but not over the phone you understand." The possibility that there could be a tap on his phone had occurred to him). "In the meantime, get used to the word on the street. In particular you're looking for a face who's been spending well on the strength of a wedge. You know the routine by now."

"They don't call me 'news' for nothing Mr Eastern, leave it with me. So, when do we make a meet? I'm gonna need some expenses."

"You'll know that a couple of hours beforehand. Just keep your bleedin' nose clean and keep your mobile handy, okay?"

Lurking in the background Joan had been listening intently to the conversation. "Well, it couldn't have been all bad, at least you were talking."

"Yeah, it's a start Joan. I just hope that when I meet Carter next, I'll be the one doing all the listening!"

In the pre-knowledge that the trial was three days hence, Eastern duly arranged the 'meet' with Carter the Saturday before, leaving the latter 48 hours to exploit his full street credibility. Come the Saturday, and full of expectancy, Eastern lost no time in contacting him again. "Carter! We're in business so I'll keep it short. I make it just coming up to 10am. That gives you two hours to rearrange your brain, the rest you know. I'll expect you no later than 12 midday, at the usual spot… be there!"

Carter was under no illusions as to the awareness of the 'rules' when their sometime plutonic association came under scrutiny. Eastern was a flesh and bone investment that he needed to study 24/7 existing as he did on illicit hand outs. Fortunately for him, as snouts come and go, Carter was classed as a unique survivor due to his uncanny tenacity to ferret out classified SP when called upon.

Assured that Joan's security was in place, Eastern exited the village on foot and headed for Preston Street via Western Road. Once there, he paused halfway down and lingered outside a doorway that was sandwiched between two restaurants. Purely out of habit he made a point of glancing both ways before entering and then proceeded to climb a set of rickety steps, eventually opening out into an office cum lounge.

Setting aside the décor the betting shop itself was no different than a hundred others in so much as you walked in, placed your first bet of the day and a couple of hours later you creep out having left your bollocks behind in the till. On entering, Eastern was forced into making an early adjustment as a pall of second hand smoke hit him between the eyes and grabbed the back of his throat. Cursing inwardly, he made a positive move towards a huddled figure locked into a racing magazine, while seated in a nearby corner.

Sensing his approach, the figure swiftly disregarded the paper and acknowledged Eastern's presence. "Mr Eastern!... guv'nor… it's been a few weeks, I…" Eastern wasn't in the mood for niceties. Any preformed ideas of a welcoming committee chaired by Carter sank without a trace as Eastern disconnected himself and went for the jugular.

"I'm only here to get a result Carter, not a flaming reference!" Breaking off he allowed a strategic look to form on his face, to set the mood. Carter gave a solid nod and indicated his intention to open up.

"So, down to business. You've gotta understand Mr Eastern, the 'street' is an open minefield at the moment all down to that conspiracy trial looming up. One minute I've got enough SP to run a headline, and an hour later it's fish and chips fodder, know what I mean?" Desperate as he was for any SP, Eastern chose to remain unruffled, in spite of Carter's negative opening gambit.

"Sure I do, so I'll settle for this morning's news and anything on top, so, what's the word?" Fifteen minutes later, and feeling slightly wiser, although £40 lighter for the privilege, he cut his way through the heaving sea of bodies and the nauseating filled environment, as he made a hasty exit for the conventional world as we know it, aside from the exclusive tones, supplied by the in-house tannoy ringing in his ears. The last thing he noted on leaving was a public notice depicting a NO SMOKING order. His reaction to it was as predictable as it gets. "The management are having a laugh. That's one bet they wouldn't want me to lay odds on!" Within seconds of hitting the outside street, the memory was wiped clean as the fresh air consumed his lungs. Lingering briefly to collect his thoughts he then headed back to Western Road.

By the time he had reached the top of Preston Street, his past £40 investment now resembled a crumpled and now defunct betting slip. Sighting an empty public call box and feeling good with his inner self, he entered a designer number which connected in seconds. Clearing his throat, he uttered the letter 'B'. Moments later a now familiar voice questioned his motive for calling.

"Ah, Mr Eastern, we had a suspicion that you might be calling in. I trust that the gamble paid off?" The doubled edged implication stunned him into silence, as the events of the last hour hit a raw nerve, causing anger to overrun mistrust.

"Say what? Listen to me you arsehole. If I thought for a minute that the tail you've obviously put on me is permanent then it all ends here. Do you understand? I don't need any bleedin' pin striped dude watching my back. That wasn't the deal. Just put me through to Rogon will you? You're seriously pissing me off." There comes a time when even spooks, it seems, succumb to pressure and are made to feel transparent from any angle, leaving Eastern to make the point, 'Hands off, I'm my own man!"

Finally a familiar voice made itself heard. "Rogon speaking, sorry about the crossed swords Mike. 'B' can be a little shit at times but leave him to me. Unfortunately it's one element that even spooks are humanised into becoming."

From feeling genuinely sane one minute and totally inadequate the next, Rogon's intervention had left Eastern briefly stranded in 'never never land' before replying: "Are you saying that my conversation was being taped?" Eastern gasped.

"Once again I apologise Mike. You should have been forewarned. Familiarity is a dirty word in the department, we prefer to use the expression 'personal scrutiny'. So naturally we all subscribe to it, basically." He went on, "We might all breathe the same air but in reality you're just another statistic amongst thousands. Locked into a disc and hidden away in a secluded vault some place."

"Shit! I wonder who I'm sharing a bed with?" Eastern quipped.

"The good news is, you'll never get to know Mike. Statistics are non-biological for that reason alone..." he countered. "Anyway, you wouldn't want to meet an ugly one would you?" At least his 'plastic' observation afforded a level plain by inciting the pair into heavy laughter. In short, a dual personification of east meets west.

Rogon then turned his attention to business as usual. "I presume this isn't just a courtesy call? I have to admit, that as the situation stands, we are at a crossroad. Even the IPCC are drowning in bureaucratic bullshit, striving to achieve a result." On that understanding, and purely out of curiosity, Eastern decided to stall on the SP he'd gleaned from Ray Carter, and instead elected to probe a possible breakthrough, albeit a political arrangement, concerning the chief of suspect held on remand for his alleged role in the DC Terry Bryant murder.

"Talking of which," Eastern prompted, "What is the present position regarding the security guard who's in custody?"

Rogon incited, "I presume we're talking about the clemency deal here?"

"Yeah the very same. I can't figure out why the press are so reluctant to issue a follow up story. Considering that the release at that time was headline, to me it poses the question, what do you know that I don't?"

Eastern frowned heavily as Rogon chuckled in reply to his request, albeit an act of cynicism on his part, before continuing their conversation. "You're nobody's fool are you Mike? I won't kid to you when I say that the deal never existed in the first place. In fact..."

Eastern's anger at being isolated jarred him into a swift intervention: "What the hell is it with you fucking people? And how long have you been holding out on me? I personally pay for certain SP fresh off the press which you in turn will get for nothing. All I get in return is a poxy brick wall thrown at me. Spooks just about sums it up for me. You people act like you're untouchable by living in a cocoon of convenience. And in case it's slipped your less than plastic mind, my bleedin' neck is also on the line here amongst others. So, you'd better come up with some answers pretty damn quick. You owe me that much."

Once a spook, always a spook. And Rogon wasn't about to decamp on the strength of a quick fire reference partnered by a verbal threat. His own induction period of brainwashing on demand was light years away. And as a political android, whatever feelings he retained could be weighed on a set of pharmaceutical scales.

As was to be expected, Rogon's attitude remained undiminished, and he responded with the fervour of a cobra on heat. "Welcome once more Mike to the league of uncivilised gentlemen, where rules are made to suit the location. That is why we are a non corruptible organisation, and personalities are rarer than a 'Penny Black'."

"I reckon I've got the message Rogon," Eastern added, in a subliminal manner, before continuing, "But let's not forget my input into this case, when the bell rings, especially where files are concerned."

"Your omission is duly noted Mike, and, if nothing else, I am a good listener."

Eastern duly went on to divulge his findings, when searching for possible leads, while spent at Division and HQ as he explained. "Overall I was connected with at least 10 files in particular, giving me cause to their validity. It soon became clear to me that certain prosecution witness statements had either been misplaced conveniently or taken while under duress. And in some cases, exhibit forensic reports appeared to be lacking in depth, mainly from a defence point of view. Going on from that, I picked up on a designer ratio of outcomes in so much that four were quashed due to 'NO CASE TO ANSWER', and the remaining six 'no guilty' pleas, were held up in lieu of an alleged convicted third party blatantly taking the rap. Once again under scrutiny, a certain set of initials sanctioning reports, namely 'SDC' appeared to be synonymous throughout. I deemed them to represent Sir Daniel Conway no less, amongst other family ties present. I can only add that if I were SDC right now, I'd be looking for a good brief. From where I'm standing, the corruption on offer makes double standards look like an optional extra."

Even Rogon himself was adamant in summing up Eastern's input. "That went better than I could have visualised Mike. Having said that, my position before and after any calculated decision that I arrive at to proceed has to be remain tenable. Our case going forward is complex and delicate to say the least. So we need to be 100% certain that our judgement is unblemished. Based on your findings, I'll contact the IPCC first before setting up a meeting extraordinary with the PM. The sooner this lousy business reaches a conclusion the better."

Pausing to reflect on a delayed after thought, Rogon chose to hone in on Eastern's previous leading enquiry about the detained security guard. "I realise that it's fresh in your mind Mike but the decision not to create 'Joe Public's interest' by feeding them with unclassified SP came directly from Whitehall and not, I hasten to add, from me."

Eastern, being on the other end of the line, would never have been aware of the quizzical look that spread on demand over Rogon's face before he concluded: "Believe it or not Mike, but even spooks are answerable to a higher authority."

A mutual agreement then briefly existed as a form of touché came into play triggered by the mocking tones of Eastern laughing due to Rogon's disclosure. It then occurred to him that the latter hadn't come up with a motive to collaborate the Government's decision to use the press as a means to an end. In the event, Eastern demanded an

A level of understanding

explanation.

Rogon, to be fair, didn't hesitate in reply by showing his keenness to talk shop. "The situation is critical enough to allow politics to enter the equation. Hence the bureaucracy shit hitting the proverbial fan. The current elected party are desperate that 'Mr Big' be removed from the system on the pretext that he's a household name, and promptly enlisted us spooks to bail them out. Surreal as it may seem, it could also be said that in a sense, bent or otherwise that particular person is holding the key to the country's political future. As you're probably aware Mike, there's a coming election on the horizon. Therefore, by jointly bringing 'Mr Big' down, it would create a massive winning party vote."

"And the opposition, what's their take on the situation?"

"As you can imagine, they're strongly opposed to the idea and are presently calling for a new reform bill to be rushed through."

"I see. Although, what about the existing law as it stands? Can you elaborate on it?"

"Not exactly Mike. It's a grey area and I don't wish to go down that road. For whatever reasons they're saying that the police should deal with their own, full stop."

Eastern, as yet, wasn't concerned, and pushed Rogon for more. "But surely the IPCC are…"

Rogon wasn't up a debate on the matter and swiftly dismissed the ongoing enquiry by cutting him short. "Mike! Listen to me. Don't get too involved, it could lead you into making the job become personal if you let it, and that's the bottom line."

In ignorance, Rogon's lacklustre advice had inadvertently ignited Eastern's fragile temperament and, in doing so, pushed it up to another level, causing a further verbal retaliation. "Personal? You need to get a life Rogon. Your plastic existence has drained you of reality. Less than 48 hours ago, while on the case, I was almost wiped out by a paid jockey on crack. I would put it to you, that more than personifies the bloody word personal! Know what I mean? Cretin!"

Question: when is a spook not a spook? In Rogon's case, in the act of placing one's foot in one's mouth and making yourself inaudible.

Having now disengaged his brain, an injection of protocol somehow filtered through by way of an appeasement. "I guess I'm becoming a martyr to apologies just lately as far as you're concerned Mike. But, if it makes you any happier, it's not all doom and gloom."

"Meaning what exactly?" Eastern fired back with a hint of reservation.

"Your failed car accident. You need to know that it hadn't gone unnoticed. In fact, it's fair to say, that the bogus driver has now been removed from the equation."

"Removed?" You could almost hear the clash of Eastern's eyebrows meeting up as his face distorted from Rogon's well timed and relaxed implication. "You could have said assassinated and saved me the bother. But thanks anyway."

The advantage of inbred diplomacy then reigned supreme as Rogon put his claim into perspective by stating in a sardonic manner: "We prefer to use the term 'eliminated from our enquiries'."

"Yeah I bet you do," Eastern muttered under his breath, but was forced to smile at the same time. "Incidentally, do I get to know the details?"

"You know better than to ask Mike. I can only add that an unidentified body has been retrieved from the water at 'C dock' in Shoreham Harbour in the early hours of this morning. Forensics are carrying out a full PM on the perpetrator's body as we speak. That way, we avoid the grief surrounding a cover up." If smiling ever became a criminal act then Eastern could possibly be looking at a 10 year stretch at Rogon's verbal coup de grace.

"I would have put you in the picture earlier, given the chance," Rogon added ruefully and continued, "For what it's worth, we found sufficient evidence on the body to support our claim in linking him as a member of the same firm accredited to the security guard on remand and the recent gun victim that I was forced to deal with myself recently."

"At least there's some form of light beginning to show at the end of the tunnel at last." Eastern commented. "And a lead as to who's pulling their strings would be the ultimate, wouldn't you say?" Whatever their love/hate relationship afforded, there was no room left for doubt as to where their role in commitment lay.

"Amen to that!" Rogon exclaimed. Their enlightening conversation soon came to a close with Rogon reminding him that the trial was due to start in two days' time, that being the forthcoming Monday. With that in mind, and confident in the knowledge that any further business allayed to Carter had been put to rest, the likelihood emerging from a relaxing weekend seemed like a good enough welcome reprieve.

Chapter Fifteen
Trial and error

On reflection the last few months had been a catastrophic roller coaster, graduating to a fear of uncertainty, stark terror and back again. Sooner or later, something was bound to give, and it wasn't so much a question of how, but when. Intensely preoccupied as he was, Eastern glanced up warily from his laptop as Joan approached him. Almost at once, a foreboding sense that something was amiss kicked in as their eyes met. In a split second, his congested mind had crossed over one parallel to form a new one and, in doing so, allowed him to reach deep into her mind.

As he suspected, it became evident there was a problem that had been festering for some time. Having said that, he then needed to reassure himself, "It could be my imagination…" he broke off suddenly, as she made to speak.

"I'm sorry Mike, I didn't mean to startle you."

Lowering his gaze, he sighed deeply and closed his laptop. "No that's fine Joan, don't apologise on my account. Although God knows I could use a break, and it goes without saying that you could use one too."

"A drink? I'll fix you a Scotch…yes, that's what I'll do." Oblivious to any notion he may have held, she headed off towards the drinks cabinet in a robotic fashion.

"Joan!" he wasn't even aware that he was shouting at her. "For

Christ's sake it's not even 10am…" pausing, he slowly lowered his voice, "Just, just leave it please." Her eyes took on a vacant look as he claimed her hand and guided her towards the nearest chair. "We really do need to talk Joan. These mood swings of late can't be allowed to continue. You have to get a grip on life, don't let go now," he implored. "You owe it to yourself Joan. You've been systematically put through the ringer these past few weeks. So I can well understand how you're feeling."

She studied his face momentarily, searching desperately for an answer. "You do?"

It was almost as if she was pleading for confirmation. His face screwed up in sympathetic rage at her self imposed demeanour. "Poor bitch, she doesn't even know what's hit her," he told himself reluctantly. "Not only that, there's the trial to contend with as well…" He spoke out loud, "Joan, I've been thinking, how do you feel about taking some leisure time out, even if it's only for a few days?"

Her face remained impassive, even her mind became set on auto as she replied in a blasé manner: "You mean Framfield and my parents don't you?"

A wave of relief surged through Eastern's body as she coincided with the crux of the matter. "As things stand it could be the ideal solution Joan. As from Monday, life around here could be hell. Besides, it's not as if you will be miles away. Plus, of course, you'll benefit security wise. So, what do you say?"

Once again her commitment to non aggression, common sense attitude, rose to his proposal and she nodded brusquely in a positive manner. "I'll phone home shortly to make some arrangements, and leave first thing in the morning."

"Great. In the meantime, I'll contact Rogon and put him in the picture." Breaking off momentarily, his shoulders rose and fell as he laughed outwardly. "That'll piss him off for a start, knowing that we've got plans of our own."

In return, Joan smiled for England, before speaking: "On reflection, your suggestion is a good idea Mike. I'm beginning to feel better already."

"In that case, I will have a drink after all darling." He was chuckling to himself as she handed him a small Scotch.

"I know it's a cliché Mike but what shall we drink to?"

Eastern retaliated almost immediately, "That has got to be the easiest question I've had to deal with all week…" Raising his glass, he exclaimed loudly, "To absent spooks, everywhere."

The following morning Eastern stood and watched until Joan's car disappeared out of sight. The look of satisfaction that masked his face became clear evidence, even at a distance as he cast his eye around the periphery of the square. He then waited a few seconds or so before announcing to the World at Large "I know you're out there Rogon. So just make sure you keep up your end of the bargain. And I'll do likewise."

Later on that morning, a fully relaxed and contented Eastern manoeuvred himself into the depths of a leather upholstered armchair and allowed his body language to do the talking for him. In spite of Joan's absence, he wasn't to be found alone. The token bottle of his favourite poison and resident ice bucket ensured him the option of being in good company. Maybe the video he'd attempted to view had lost its appeal or maybe his Scotch had inadvertently developed a hidden talent. He was in a semi comatose state one minute and then subjected to what reality had to offer the next. "A baptism of fire," he thought as he fought to shrug off the relentless tone now sounding off from his landline expressing a desire to be part of his world.

"Please God that's Joan and not bleedin' Rogon," he remarked selfishly. "She's probably called to let me know that she's arrived and settled in okay." Any other thoughts that he may have held bearing on anticipation disintegrated as the familiar unfeeling tones issuing from Rogon's voice invaded his space.

"Mike? Yes, you've guessed it's me. And before you say anything, you need to know that minutes after leaving Brunswick Square I had a security guard positioned on Joan's case. Basically, I need to know whether or not she has made contact with you say, in the last hour or so?" An uneasy silence reigned as Eastern's fuddled brain became swamped with opposing scenarios. It became clear to him that Rogon's leading omission stank of a personal guilt trip. Leaving himself desperately seeking some solid answers in lieu of a debate on Rogon's security priorities.

"You've got some bleedin' nerve Rogon! It's a Saturday night for fucksake! So I'm not in the market for your poxy mind games. Forget the verbal crap and get straight to the point. Oh, while you were at it, and just for the record, I haven't received a call all day. The only contact I've had concerned you this morning over security."

If Rogon was anticipating something more positive out of Eastern's backlash then he was quick to realise that he was on a hiding to nothing. The only bullet he had left to fire was now saturated with the truth of the matter as he pulled the verbal trigger to expose the real meaning relating to his call. His curt reply, when it came, was brief and cut to the chase: "In that case, I fear we have a problem Mike."

Eastern's brain immediately switched to red alert as Rogon's suspect omission concerning security came back to haunt him, only this time with a vengeance as Joan channelled into his thoughts. "Why do I get the feeling that you're about to piss me right off? If anything untoward has happened to her I'm holding you personally responsible Rogon. So I strongly advise you to offload what SP you have got on your mind right now!" As requests go, it wasn't worth the air space as Rogon picked up from where he left off.

"The crux of the matter is, I'm not in a position to do that Mike. As I said before, I'm rather hoping that you know something I don't. Frankly, unintentionally or otherwise, she has given my man the slip. Hence the call." Patience was at a premium, and Eastern had enough to convince himself that their conversation had now run dry.

"I suggest you hang up Rogon, I'll take over from here. Please God she's in control of the situation. Joan's had her fair share of grief just lately. Incidentally, you might as well contact your man and tell him to back off, seeing as I intend taking over from here. One other thing before you go... Where was the last sighting of her that we can be sure of?"

"Apparently going into a Superstore, for whatever reason, situated on the edge of the city in the Hollingbury locale, according to my man. Unfortunately, that's where the surveillance all fell apart." With nothing more to add, their speculative conversation folded forthwith.

Anxious as he was to unravel the sudden disappearance of Joan, the notion that a possible abduction could have taken place was never far away in Eastern's mind."

"Mind you," he quickly reminded himself. "The fact that Joan wasn't even a witness in the forthcoming trial would mean she would serve no beneficial purpose, should it happen, thus rendering any ulterior motive as being as misguided action." His next impulse was to contact Joan's parents on a pretext that she may have been in touch or indeed arrived at Framfield. From the moment that his call was acknowledged he sensed that his timing, giving further consideration could have been handled more effectively, in knowing that their relationship had moved on somewhat surpassing a client status.

Drumming his fingers on a nearby coffee table in a gesture of impatience unexpectedly caught him on the back foot in dealing with the dulcet tones of protocol colliding with his own disposition. Mrs Travers' opening enquiry came to an abrupt end, consequently placing her on the receiving end, as Eastern cut in: "Is Joan there with you? If she is, I really need to talk to her, it's important. Oh, and in case you hadn't guessed already this is Mike Eastern speaking and concerned about Joan's present wellbeing."

Fortunately for him, class will always out, forcing Eastern into humble submission. As Mrs Travers retaliated, echoing her own thoughts on the situation. She made it quite clear that no contact had been made at that point and should it arise, he would be the first to be made aware. Eastern then apologised for this openness and stated he would endeavour to contact Joan post haste. They hung up.

To the best of his knowledge, Eastern estimated that Joan was about an hour overdue from her expected arrival to Framfield which, on reflection, caused him to doubt her mother's somewhat carefree attitude allayed to her absence. Two outgoing calls inside of fifteen minutes and a stored message in reply to nothing began to eat away at his frustration. "It's the poxy not knowing that makes it worse. Just what the hell is stopping her from making contact? It's totally out of character and the relevance is pissing me off!" Even Rogon, for reasons of his own, seemed impervious to his plight, by keeping his own exclusive distance.

The breakthrough to his problem when it materialised proved to be totally unexpected. Later on that evening, and by way of a third party source, Eastern discovered an envelope lying on his doormat prior to locking up for the night. It was simply addressed 'MIKE', set in capitals, thus making the handwriting unrecognisable. His initial reaction, conjecture apart, was one of overwhelming relief. Feverishly, he tore the flap open and hastily removed the contents. Subsequently, his worst fears were dispelled, as the type of handwriting, and the message it signified became apparent.

Dear Mike,

First and foremost I feel I have to apologise for my actions, including the stress that this must have caused you. Please believe me when I say that I never set out to upset our personal arrangement, and that the present outcome has no bearing on our private life, which I cherish dearly. At this point, you will be pleased to know, that I am safe and well and able to relax in a convenient atmosphere of my own choice. The decision confronting me didn't come easy, although, under the circumstances, it was a necessary one. (I refer to the trial and the added grief we have shared.) It was heartbreaking not being able to return your call in knowing that Rogon and his damn spooks were never far away. Just for once, my present address is our secret, and ours alone! I've included a contact number for you as well. We can talk some more tomorrow, say at 10 o clock in the morning. I have also been in touch with my parents, so they are fully aware of my position and I have their overwhelming backing. Things will become clearer tomorrow my darling, trust me?

Until then, all my love, Joan x

Mike Eastern now had a problem. But hell! He wasn't about to complain. The expression registered on his face evoked more depth from inner feeling than the contents emerging from the letter he was holding. For the second time, he felt compelled to absorb the genuine rights to Joan's written confessional, while attempting to make a case for her for displaying the obvious strength of affection that she indubitably felt toward him. Needless to say, he failed miserably, but felt good in doing so all the same. In the time it had taken him to grasp the situation, his whole world had suddenly turned on its axis and, in doing so, unleashed other hidden worlds to spin out of control in his head, each individual one then colliding and harmlessly exploding on impact while in unison to a new and updated heartbeat. Without realising it, an abandoned motive suddenly found a voice.

"God! I haven't felt this way in years." He exclaimed loudly. "I guess I get the chance for another bite of the proverbial apple…yeah, why not?" if he'd thought for a minute that he could well be in for a sleepless night, it would have been the one remaining factor he could have banked on. In spite of everything, he did manage to grab a couple of hours even though they were systematically tainted with bias dreams.

Western Road Brighton on a Sunday morning is no different to the slow lane of the M25 on any given weekday, bodies apart that is. Having just exited a newsagents, Eastern glanced across the road and made an immediate beeline to the one remaining empty telephone booth situated at the top of Russell Square. His watch was saying 9.55am but his thoughts were somewhere else. Even the dialling tone became music to his ears long before the familiar sound of Joan's voice came into play.

"Hi Mike, I guessed it had to be you by your timing alone. You obviously found my letter."

"You bet I did Joan. But what the hell is going on? I didn't know what to think. I can only presume that you're staying in London, going by the number you enclosed."

"That's right," she echoed. "In fact I'm staying at Toni's flat in Bloomsbury, would you believe? I contacted her last night after having made my decision to give Framfield a miss. Luckily for me, it turned out, that she was in Hove for a couple of days, covering an assignment for a magazine."

"So you obviously met up at some point then, before heading on to London?" He swore that he could hear Joan laugh in the background, before replying.

"Always the PI, Mike? I need to teach you how to relax more often. Having said that, you're right of course. I contacted Toni, minutes after having the pleasure of ditching Rogon's security spook. After which, I drove back to her place in Hove, where I wrote the letter explaining my sudden turnaround. Toni then gave me a spare key to her Bloomsbury flat. Shortly after that, I left knowing that she would deliver the letter for me, as I instructed." Together they continued to talk at length on various aspects which included Eastern's insistence that any foreseeable planning would become a joint venture.

From the short time that he'd taken to hang up and exit the booth the sun had decided on making a guest appearance, breaking through the overhead cloud. The immediate effect became all the impetus that he needed as he turned on his heel and headed back the opposite way to Churchill Square via a particular 'brunch bar' to relax over a coffee…or so he thought. Having selected a prime viewing window table encompassing the full vista in sight, it was left to the impromptu and melodic tones from his mobile to crash his private space.

He didn't require a second glance at the name occupying his screen to confirm that the symbol 24/7 was etched in granite and went hand in hand with a public health warning. Grudgingly he made the contact, but ensured that he held the rights to any verbal pecking order. "Where the hell do you get off Rogon? It's fucking Sunday morning for Christ sake. You need to get yourself a life moron." His outburst was breath wasted on Rogon's Government emotional implants.

"Mike, good morning to you. Listen, I need to get you up to speed. Basically, we are rescheduling your position within the agency due to imposed pressure from upstairs. Yesterday I was summoned to an extraordinary meeting held at Downing Street relating to crucial talks with the PM about tomorrow's trial." From then on, Eastern could only listen in as a robot spectator whilst Rogon droned on avidly, stipulating his instructions with the protocol associated with his new role.

Rogon explained: "Ideally we are looking to get a new body in on the inside to be in a position to be able to mingle freely amongst the 'silks', plus of course the gallery. The fact that you're presently alienated from the agency by arrangement means of course that you will be subjected to an ID crisis at some point. Nevertheless, it goes without saying that certain internal steps have been put in place to ensure that your cover doesn't get blown."

From the minute that Rogon had asserted his one man verbal assault, it had left Eastern struggling to play catch up. The mere thought of 10.30am on a Sunday morning combined with a no nonsense directive issued by a figure bearing a statistical name had about as much future as an underwater wax candle! In summing up, Eastern left his counterpart under no illusions as to his proposed new post.

"Hold it right there Rogon, when I decide to come on board, it suited me by doing the establishment a favour. Not as a flaming career, my pension lies elsewhere. Do I make myself clear?"

It soon became apparent that the main difference between a spook and a lack of communication is that there is no difference, mainly due to the overriding lack of interpretation. Unfortunately Rogon was a past master when it came to 'mind games'. "That's what I like about you Mike; you always say what you are thinking. It's the one remaining trait that certain people are gifted with. Me? I'm just a by product of brainwashed Government fodder. But that was my decision, so regrets do not exist in my vocabulary. You, on the other hand are a born natural, and I admire your tenacity in the role that we share. Like it or not, there's a job to be done, meaning that I would rather work with you, than against you... good man. Now that we have an understanding going, here's what I intend."

He then blissfully went on talking shop, leaving a somewhat disillusioned and bemused Eastern dangling on the end of a line while waiting to catch his breath. Before concluding, Rogon stamped his call by declaring that 'B' would be contacting him at his flat around midday for a short briefing regarding the importance of his presence when officiating at Crown Court. Long before his coffee had become dregs, Eastern had decided to throw in the towel by granting Rogon a hollow victory on the basis that it is better the devil you know.

He then concluded that "At the very least I owe it to Joan to finish what we had both started."

The word 'frustration' was fast becoming an epidemic when it applied to parking a car. Leading up to that point, Eastern's preparation had been flawless. Unfortunately, a huge police presence within Lewes and the periphery of the court house had ideas of their own, notably,

"Would you mind moving along sir? I suggest that you use the station car park." A short while later a seriously pissed off Eastern cursed Rogon and the world at large. With every step he made his censored way back up the steep hill leading to the high street and salvation.

"Fuck you Rogon! And your definition of a low profile, I'm nearly on my poxy knees."

The idea that life could only get better was once again put to the test by the trauma arising from an identity crisis when attempting to gain admission to the main court room. Thankfully the stairs leading up to the public gallery offered little resistance. For the first time since he'd vacated the flat that morning, he finally felt that he had arrived. Heaving with relief and the use of his warrant card, he managed to secure a front row seat overlooking counsel's 'chicken run'. Glancing downwards, a sudden surge of warm air carried on a vibrant wave of mixed emotional voices and intermingled bodies rose up from ground zero and by doing so systematically consumed his body. The atmosphere, in contrast, became electric and he felt that he could almost reach out and touch it.

Striving to adjust his vision, he desperately attempted to scan a sea of faces, hoping to locate a pocket of recognition that would possibly tie him in with the ongoing investigation. Disappointment was no substitute for initiative, and concluding by reminding himself that 'it's still early days as yet and the best is yet to come. Sooner or later something will give and when it does, I'll be raising my game... that's a promise." It wasn't long before the public and the press media alike became distanced from their own singular version of events towards the case by being drawn into a sense of reality as the Sessions got under way. Flanked and handcuffed by two burly officers, DCI Conway then became the first prisoner to make an appearance in the dock, closely followed by two other co-defendants both of whom were linked to the forthcoming alleged charges per se.

From his strategic position, Eastern felt riveted to the lowly figure of Conway, who in spite of his self induced status, still managed to display a show of facial arrogance when acknowledging his counsel. Switching his gaze, Eastern endeavoured to catch Conway's eye with his own as they bored deep inside his frame while inciting his mind to release associate thoughts of his own. "Make the most of it you mindless loser, and while you are at it think of Andy Dowling and remember this, what goes around comes around and long before this trial is over, 'karma' will surface and be available to bite your arse!"

The distinctive overtones from the melodic voice of the chief clerk requesting the court to all rise, cut short any prophetic views Eastern may have held. Just then, the presiding Judge entered the room and took his seat, leaving the accused to remain still standing in the dock. Moments later, their identities were confirmed and noted, allowing the clerk to submit the charges that were laid against them. In reply, a plea of 'not guilty' was entered by Conway, as opposed to a decisive 'guilty' from the other two defendants.

For his part, Eastern was stunned into silence as an unexpected gasp of disbelief rippled around the court room at Conway's audacious defence plea. Further proceedings were observed but not before opposing counsels were summoned to the bench for a spontaneous reminder on ethics, bearing in mind the severity of the case. And then it became 'theatre time' as the opening speech curtain went up. Eastern closed his eyes and allowed his mind to obtain Carte Blanche to a private beach, anywhere, in a vain attempt to escape the predictable verbal lines of action as the prosecuting counsel carved out a case against Conway in an intimidating manner, as he addressed the jury.

Meanwhile Eastern had discovered utopia. The inviting jug of iced cool sangria lapping between a cocktail of fruit suddenly faded into obscurity along with the miles of sun kissed sandy beaches. A sense of feeling that he wasn't on his own, flooded his mind and washed over his befuddled sub conscious causing him to start. Grimacing he rubbed his eyes cursing as he did so in the knowledge that reality was more than a state of one's mind and right now could be found alive and kicking under duress inside his body. "…and so I say to you, do not be taken in by the fact…" the pleading voice emerging from the prosecutor then came back to haunt him, as he continued to brainwash the jury on an overdose of unbiased facts.

"God Almighty! Doesn't the guy know when to stop? He must have been gabbling on for the last 30 minutes or so."

"Actually, it's been almost an hour, and you're right. Personally,

I get the impression that the man thinks he's on a film set." Without realising it, Eastern's comments had been picked up on by a stranger sitting alongside him. Instinctively, he whirled round to face him.

"I'm sorry, I..."

"Don't be." The stranger intervened and continued: "I get the distinct impression that you don't want to be here any more than I do. Quite honestly, I think the verdict when it comes will be a foregone conclusion." Eastern's interest in his chosen remark became aroused by seducing him into thinking that there was more going on behind his comment than suggested. His intention to pursue their spontaneous conversation at arm's length became appropriately well timed, as the defence counsel called for a short recess to deliberate on a specific statement. Initially the plea was heavily rebuked by the judge, who then went on to hand out a lesson in preparation to counsel, before finally agreeing.

Fired up, and acting like a cat on a hot tin roof, Eastern decided to make the first move by making his intentions known. "I think that if the truth is known, the judge is as bored as you and me. Anyway, I think I'll stretch my legs and grab a coffee at the same time, how about you?" His remark broke the ice and caused the stranger to laugh.

"Guilty as charged your Lordship, by the way my name's Granger... Paul Granger that is." He then proffered his hand for Eastern to shake. Without hesitation, Eastern shook it warmly.

"Mike Eastern, I'm pleased to know you." At least their resumed conversation had more going for it than the so called coffee. Eastern lowered his cup and quipped "I can't see that getting past the local fraud squad without a good brief." Once again Granger laughed and went on to probe.

"So, what's your interest in this case then Mike, personal or professional?" Simple enough question, providing of course that your name isn't Mike Eastern. He was forced to hesitate, as a mental picture of Rogan took up residence in his subconscious, waving a banner of security.

"That's a good question Paul." Hedging to gain some thinking time was coming at a price. The importance of security had entered the equation. Fortunately, Granger inadvertently put him out of his misery.

"I'm not surprised by the amount of press media on show when you consider the gravity of the case, myself included. It was beginning to look like a reporters' seminar in the foyer at one point." Eastern's ears instantly pricked up at Granger's free omission as to his line of business.

"I had a feeling that your genre lay in that direction." It then became a ploy on his part to draw Granger in. "I notice that you're not displaying your ID tag, any reason why?" A quizzical look began to form on his face before replying.

"If I didn't know you better Mike, I'd have marked you down as a copper." He chuckled.

"So you are attached to the press then?" Eastern elected to go for bust.

"Yes! In a manner of speaking. I'm a freelance journalist, mainly local stuff. After 20 odd years working in Fleet Street, this is a bloody holiday. Having said that, any personal interest I hold is with Conway." Stopping short, he continued in a dismissive manner with a negative shake of the head. "But that's another story, so there you have it."

"Please...please go on Paul, I'm more than interested in what you have to say."

"Yeah, well, as I say, I still retain my press card hence my admission, although I leave the headlines to the big boys. Mind you, I still manage to thieve a living in spite of that, but like it or not my game is about connections. So you see," he added, "The bottom line for me means that from a passport to a pension, if you know what I mean?" His demeanour then went off at a tangent. "By the way, you never did state your business." Regrettably Eastern now found himself caught flatfooted in midstream. Going with the tide he swiftly decided would be his best option, rather than reveal his legitimate persona.

"Let us just say that I have a legal addiction where crime is concerned, and leave it at that if you don't mind?" Seemingly satisfied, Granger was then left to draw his own conclusions. And from then on, their conversation drifted back onto the relevance of the case. For his part Eastern was eager to digress on a personal point of view previously raised. "My interest is with the accused namely Conway." Yes I'm sure that's how you put it, I'm intrigued by the fact that you went into denial when I raised the subject previously."

Momentarily, Granger appeared to be taken aback by the suddenness of the enquiry, although he had no qualms in discussing his past revelation. The reaction on Granger's part when it came was almost one of total relief.

"No shit! I had a gut feeling that you were about to bring Conway back into the equation. He's been hovering in the back of my mind for some time now." There extempore conversation as then curtailed by the voice of the court usher alerting them to the fact that the trial would shortly be in session. A fired up Eastern had alternative ideas, by wanting more from their discussion.

"Look! Just a suggestion Paul. How do you feel about grabbing an early lunch? Quite honestly, I don't think we are going to miss much, it being the opening day. I'd appreciate your time if we could continue where we both left off...what do you say?"

Granger didn't hesitate and nodded his approval. "And a decent coffee to go with it. I know a place we can use, it's only a few minutes away, just off the high street." Five minutes later, they made the café their own.

"Ah, this is more like it." Eastern made himself comfortable and caught the waitress's attention. In no time at all, they picked up where they had previously left off. "So, what alerted you to forming an opinion in the first place Paul?"

"Let's see now. Yeah it was something I came across some years ago, when I was reporting for what was then the Oxford Mail. In addition to the field work, I was obliged to maintain and keep certain files up to scratch...proofing headlines...media arts...advertising, that sort of thing."

"Blimey, you make it sound like a labour of love." Eastern suggested.

"On the contrary Mike, my role became more of a learning curve, bearing in mind that I had access to headlines prior to publishing."

"And your point being?"

"Intrigue, one article in particular that caught my attention, concerned a report engulfing a local protection racket operating at that time. It was eventually solved by the police, and get this, the arresting officer was DS Conway would you believe?"

"No kidding? I can see where this is heading." Chimed in Eastern.

"Anyway, you can imagine. At that time, it was quite a coup for a small paper, especially knowing that the tabloids would have paid good money for the same exposure. Anyway, a couple of hours prior to running with the story, it was conveniently removed from print and substituted with a down grade on a washing line thief! Would you believe? I obviously questioned the editor's decision, and consequently wound up being severely reprimanded in the process. Eastern meanwhile, had trouble to contain himself.

"Why do I get the feeling that there's a good end to this story?"

"You're not wrong mate, and it only gets better. A week or so later and purely by chance I came across a defunct company paying in book, abandoned in a waste bin. The last stub I noticed had no banker's recognition stamp on it, and somebody had made a bad job of erasing the amount of money entered on it."

"Uhm, the story stinks already, so what amount of money are we talking about here?" Granger was now on a roll and singing like a proverbial canary.

"After much scrutiny, I arrived at a figure in excess of £2,000, which at that time was a lot of dough. And it didn't come from selling newspapers, that's for sure. My first instinct linked the money with the cancellation of the late headline, due to a nasty smell being circulated at the time concerning local corruption. Nothing was proved, I hasten to add, but I still stand by my convictions regarding the rumours aimed at the police. Incidentally, it's important to remember that I didn't have a clue who DS Conway was at the time, except to say that his father was also serving in the same branch as a senior officer. Now years later, the past has come back to haunt me, by reminding me that his son is now in spitting distance of me."

Eastern continued to press for more. "So, when you saw his name appear once again on this latest bung charge, you just put two and two together? That's unbelievable, I'm struggling to take your story in Paul. I'm lost for words, it doesn't come any better than this."

Granger's eyes lit up as he murmured quietly, "Oh but it does Mike!" Granger stressed, "I managed to hang on to that delinquent cheque stub and I reckon someone would pay an awful lot of dough just to get their hands on something as high profile as that! Don't you think?"

"Think?" Granger's open revelation climaxed inside Eastern's brain causing him to explode. "I'll tell you what I think. Do you realise the enormity of what we are dealing with here? As evidence goes, that stub book has to be on a par with 'Pandora's Box'. Opening it up could finally expose the vital link between Conway and 'Mr Big' himself. As evidence goes, it has to be gilt edged."

"You've lost me Mike, I'm a bit out of my depth here."

"On the contrary Paul, you nailed the problem yourself, when you stated that Conway was joined to his father's hip. Working on the assumption that we're both right, their charismatic association all those years ago had to be the start of a conspired double act, culminating into this latest expose."

"Hell! In retrospect, I wanted to say that myself, but I didn't have the bollocks. What really concerns me is how in God's name has his father managed to stay undetected all this time? From where I'm sitting his attachment damn well stinks." Rapt in their own discrete conclusions, Eastern momentarily allowed his direction to go off at a tangent.

"How indeed? Even Rogon would be out on a limb deducing an answer to that one."

"Rogon?" Instantaneously Granger found himself temporarily isolated, and somewhat baffled. "I'm sorry, I'm not familiar with the name. Should I be?" Aware of his sudden faux pas caused Eastern to quietly chuckle to himself.

"Forget it Paul…it was a lousy mistake, and please God you never get involved with this man." Taking note was the easy part, Granger's body language registered the effects deriving from a roller coaster bound on a cocaine trip.

"So, where the hell do I go from here? I mean, this changes everything. With the right make up I could be looking at the 'scoop' of the year. And as for the money side…"

"Whoa! Hold it right there Paul…it's imperative that you listen and learn." His positive intervention luckily backed Granger into a corner, forcing him to hear Eastern out. The moment then became surreal, as

Eastern himself unwittingly found himself facing a dilemma of huge consequences allayed to his cover persona. The moment was right when thinking on his feet by appeasing Granger, while at the same time, endeavouring to keep his true identity under wraps. Or, at least until he found it necessary to abort his man identity charade. "Playing the situation down to redeem some thinking time would be the way forward," he convinced himself.

"Coffee! How about you? Personally I could murder another one. I figure that we both need to reconcile some of the relevant facts concerning the flip side to the problem, long before you rush headlong into the unknown, right?" Granger nodded eagerly to signify his approval and appeared to be relaxed as Eastern signalled his intention to reorder.

Having secured his coffee Eastern became the first to break their silence.

"Funny thing."

"Say what?"

"Life I guess. Oh sorry, I was just thinking out loud. An hour or so ago I didn't know you from Mickey Mouse and now here we are attempting to deal with a forensic time bomb! It's crazy!" His frankness was now shared by Granger's willingness to accept that his undisclosed 'find' could possibly rebound on him, simply by not pursuing the right channels.

"Fucksake! It's that significant eh?"

"I can't stress the fact enough, you have to believe it Paul."

"I can live with that, the question is, where do we go from here?"

"We..." Eastern demanded. "Don't! That is until I make an impromptu phone call. You wait here. I won't be long."

Wearing a phased look, Granger nodded and replied, "You are one bloody mystery Mike, I'm having a problem with your day job and who you really are!"

Smiling broadly Eastern left him to dangle unreservedly: "That's for me to know and you to find out Paul. Not that you would believe me if I told you." Turning on his heel, he made his way to the gents. He was smiling as he made the desired connection. "Rogon? We need to talk. It's urgent. Something of interest has cropped up. I want you to arrange a meeting extraordinary revolving around a third party involvement."

When replying to Eastern's request, Rogon acted in his usual bland and moronic trademark: "If you insist Mike. I presume by your reasoning, it could make a viable contribution to the bung case. And yes, I'll make all the necessary arrangements." His reply was short but brief.

"Fine. Let's say 7.30 at my place tonight then."

"Leave it with me. By the way, who's your new found friend?" The innocuous enquiry was no more than Eastern had expected coming from Rogon, and he promptly cut him short. Having said that, he still continued to smile as he returned to the table.

"That went rather well by the look of it." Granger ventured.

"Yeah, please God it stays that way. Incidentally Paul, what are you doing tonight?"

Chapter Sixteen
Crime by order

The carriage clock situated on the mantelpiece was approaching 6.55pm, just as Eastern entered his lounge, closely followed by an uneasy looking Paul Granger. Sensing his apparent demeanour, Eastern motioned towards an adjacent 'mini bar' in one corner. "Feel free to help yourself Paul, and make it a large one. I've got a notion it will be a long night."

Timing just happened to be one trait that he could safely rely on, in knowing that Rogon was a martyr to that particular cause. Having downed the remains of his Scotch, his door bell alerted him to the fact that the agency had kept their part of the bargain as the clock in the lounge chimed 7.30pm exactly. Eastern had briefed Granger on the code of ethics surrounding the meet. Nevertheless, the latter appeared to be somewhat daunted by the whole process, once their blindfolds were removed at spooks HQ. Turning to Eastern, he expressed his pent up feelings. "I'm finding it hard to believe this is really happening Mike. You wouldn't want to upset these people would you? Nobody would ever find your body again!" Not wishing to elaborate on the subject, Eastern wisely decided to string him along.

"Let's just say that it wouldn't be your body lying in the coffin, if it was ever exhumed. But at least you would have had a funeral in part." The interrogation unit became instantly recognisable to Eastern as they were ushered inside by two burly departmental spooks, both of whom were instantly dismissed. It became clear to him that apart from Rogon and Granger, they were alone in the room. "Who needs people?" he mused. "there's probably more bugs secreted in these walls than a second hand mattress."

His train of thought was then shattered as Rogon greeted the pair. "Mike! Good to see you, and I presume that you must be Paul Granger…interesting." Verbal intimidation went with the territory, leaving Eastern to swiftly return his dud comment.

"You can cut out the mind games Rogon; it only gets interesting as you so indelicately put it, if you can use what I have on offer. By the way, where is 'B', shouldn't he have a say in the matter?"

Rogon shook his head in a patronising manner before replying: "Touché Mike, there's no fooling you, is there? I always maintained that you would make a damn good spook. As for 'B', he's unfortunately tied up at the present, putting a coup down in Africa so I'm led to believe."

"What!" Eastern retorted, "Not on his own surely?" Rogon was his own forthright self as usual.

"Well, not unless you call a mini arsenal including a Government Issue Barrett M107 as company… then no! From what I gather, his 'mark' is an assassination assignment and I'm sure he'll manage. He hasn't let us down yet." he expressed dolefully. Briefly Eastern closed his eyes on an impulse as he digressed.

"And to think you led me to believe that the guy was a fucking caretaker." For his part, Granger elected to sit down, presumably due to a posture complaint. Rogon then took the initiative by exercising his patience.

"Well gentlemen, what have you got for me that is so important it can't wait? I only hope that it's substantial. This case has been dragging on too long, a breakthrough at this juncture would be comforting and at the same time enable me to keep the PM off my back." Eastern then proceeded to draw up a seat and make himself comfortable. Produced a sealed plastic bag, he removed the contents and gave it to Rogon for scrutiny, who in turn made a meagre effort to study what was on offer.

"So?" Eastern enquired impatiently, "What do you make of that?" Taking into account his position, a look of unconcern crossed his face.

"Uhm, obviously a defunct bog standard PIB (paying in book). And an old one at that, I haven't come across one like this for years."

"Don't piss me off Rogon, this evidence is relevant to the case." Granger reacted to Eastern's show of temperament, by beginning to squirm in his seat at the thought of a backlash.

"No! I'm serious Mike." Rogon continued, "The day I sold my body to the state, any personal effects I carried became Government property. So what is so special about this one that it warrants a three man discussion?" Acting under Eastern's direction, Granger unfolded the story relating to the origin of the PIB. Meanwhile, Rogon sat poker faced listening intently, before passing judgement.

"I hear what you both say and indeed where it could possibly lead to." He paused, "Trouble is, it's riddled with circumstantial evidence all based on assumption. It just won't wash, I'm sorry Mike but that's how I see it."

"Utter bullshit!" Eastern wasn't about to be fobbed off having come this far. "The editor, what about the editor? If we can track him down and lean on him, there's a good chance we may be able to prove that bung money had been laundered from the proceeds via Conway's protection rackets that were prominent at the time."

Rogon was adamant in his reply. "how do we know that the guy still exists or not? And even if he was still alive and we subpoena him, he'll make the term 'no comment' more popular than a bachelor flat in the Maldives! Assuming of course that you could even find him." Eastern was still insistent on getting something out of the discussion.

"I hope that we can at least agree that finding a common link between what we have got thus far surrounding 'Mr Big', AKA Conway senior, is absolutely crucial."

"That was never in doubt Mike." Rogon confirmed. "So why do I get this feeling that you're hatching something in that head of yours? Because if you are I'd much prefer it to be unclassified information." He then turned his attention on to Granger. "Unfortunately, it all ends here for you I'm afraid and I thank you for your participation. The PIB, of course, now becomes state property." Extending his property, the two exchanged a token handshake. Granger looked almost relieved that he was allowed to go, but not before shaking Eastern's hand warmly.

"I'll keep in touch Mike if you don't mind; you never know I might just get a 'scoop' hot enough to retire on." His parting shot caused them both to chuckle.

"Amen to that Paul, as far as I'm concerned your names written all over it, isn't that so Rogon?" Nodding robotically, the latter was forced to agree. Just then, a spook agent entered the room and proceeded to blindfold Granger. Having reminded him of his allegiance to the Official Secrets act, he was then whisked away.

"And then there were two," remarked Rogon dryly before continuing, "You're in the chair now Mike, how do you propose we go about nailing Conway?" Eastern leaned forward on the table and allowed his elbows to take his weight. Prior to speaking, he stared intently at Rogon for a few seconds in a mood of deliberation as if to justify his reasoning. Coolly and calmly, he allowed one pre-set word to escape his lips; the effect of which caused Rogon to sit bolt upright.

"Blackmail!" Stunned into silence, and forced to struggle with the implication, it was left to Eastern to lower him down gently. "In a legal sort of fashion, you understand."

"How in God's name do you condone that as an undertaking for a brief?" spluttered Rogon.

"On hindsight that's the easy part, especially if the intended victim happens to be Conway senior. I've said it before Rogon, if you want big, then you have to think big."

"I wouldn't dispute that Mike, but c'mon, blackmail? You've got to be kidding me? One of us has lost the plot and from where I'm sitting you have to be a prime candidate. Having said that, I admire your nerve." Brushing his remark to one side, only ignited the strong belief that Eastern felt, regarding the credibility to his claim.

"That is your opinion but to explain my theory I need to digress. Long before and after I came on the scene, you and your agency have done all the running, and for what? I…"

Rogon was on home turf and he didn't need a progress assassination from somebody like Eastern holding a 'maverick' degree. He then cut him short.

"Blast you Mike! Don't tell me how to run my department. Thus far, we have managed to nail three 'bent' coppers."

"Need I remind you Rogon. It's how you finish, not how you start that counts." He fired back. It takes a good man to know when he's beat, and Rogon applauded his gamesmanship.

"You've got some bollocks Mike, I'll give you that. Now then, about this theory of yours, you were saying?"

"Simply don't run anymore."

"Is that it?"

"Far from it. You allow 'Mr Big' to do it all for you...call it role reversal strategy if you like, by forcing him to come to you."

If he was convinced by his logic, then Rogon didn't show it. "Just like that eh? And what do you propose I use for a contact number?" He replied acidly.

Blanking his show of witticism, Eastern spelt it out for him in no uncertain terms. "I'm only going to say it once more for your benefit Rogon. As I stated in the beginning, the answer is simply 'blackmail."

"So you said Mike, but who and what do we use as bait? And, let's not forget, at this moment in time we can't legally hang a damn thing on him. Plus, of course, who's to say the guy is bent anyway?"

Eastern was done with pussy footing around, and allowed his temperament to raise the stakes. "That's total bollocks Rogon and you know it. That arsehole is hiding behind a blanket position to remain untouchable. But not in my book. I intend to blow his cover apart, besides which I've nothing to lose. And that is our biggest asset. Doing things my way will decide whether he's bent or not. If he's legal, then he's got nothing to worry about...and me? I'm just another crank and I can live with that." Basically, the moment had now become a question of make up your mind time. So, had Eastern struck a chord?

Rogon brought his clenched fist hard down on the table top. "It's crazy! Everything about it is telling me that the idea is crazy. But you're right, it could work and I'm in. you have obviously got a game plan Mike, so lay it on me." Eastern suggested that they instigate an obligatory check as to whether the editor in Granger's submission could still possibly be alive, and, if so, bring him to book. In Rogon's case they could construct a letter of implication, the contents of which show the bearer as having retained key knowledge to Conway's participation, in subversive underground movements.

As Eastern said, "If he responds to the bait on offer, he'll inadvertently shoot himself in the foot by granting us a case on a plate. Then, as a bonus, we could always introduce the editor into our claim. And who knows, he could well save us a lot of grief by locating the guy for us." In winding up, he stressed the facts from a gambler's point of view. "Theoretically, we have got nothing to lose whatsoever. And at the same time, be safe in the knowledge that there won't be any comebacks on the agency's part in knowing that our position is watertight."

Seemingly satisfied, any existing tension voluntarily eradicated itself. Eastern remained at the HQ long enough to arrange a further meeting to finalise their way forward. In his absence, another agent was allocated his role at the ongoing trial. It was nearing 10.30pm that same evening before the agency car got round to dropping Eastern off at Brunswick Square. Leaving any thoughts he may have held in contacting Joan to one side he reassured himself "I'm pretty sure she'll understand it's the damn business I'm in." Needless to say, the 'mini bar' took the brunt of his frustration, before deciding that bed would be a better proposition than a headache to contend with.

In the event, his conclusion wouldn't have made the slightest difference as headaches have a mind of their own, by showing up when they feel like it. The 'headache' in question kicked off at HQ the following morning. Somewhat relaxed, Eastern leaned forward on the table and attempted to pour himself a coffee. Halfway through, he stalled as a grim faced Rogon entered the room. Sensing an immediate problem, Eastern decided to make the first move. "Good morning to you too!"

The reply on offer was curt and straight to the point. "Is it? Huh, not from where I'm bloody standing. I've had better ones."

Hesitating to answer, Eastern finished pouring his coffee, not wishing to be drawn into personality conflict.

He then looked up and remarked nonchalantly, "Sorry, you were saying?"

"I've just received a call from Division that I could have well done without."

"Is it something that we need to talk about?"

"I'm afraid it's become inevitable seeing as it concerns the both of us. It would appear that there's been a murder right here on our doorstep." At first Eastern became conscious that the emphasis on 'us' could be misconstrued as being personal.

"Murder you say…who…when?"

Pulling a chair up, a gaunt looking Rogon opened up. "From what we know at this juncture, the crime was carried out in the early hours of this morning. And I'm sorry to say that the victim, by all accounts, happens to be Paul Granger." Shockwaves riveted him to the chair, leaving Eastern momentarily speechless. Meanwhile, Rogon was forced to continue where he'd left off.

"Apparently it seems that a cleaner came across his body this morning, and alerted the police. From what I can gather, the Path boys are examining the body as we speak and early indications leave them to suspect that cause of death was by strangulation."

Eastern had now sufficiently recovered from Rogon's explosive disclosure. "There has to be a mistake surely, I mean, think about it? It was only a few hours ago that the three of us were sitting here talking. No, I don't buy it. To my mind, the police have fouled up, it's obviously a case of mistaken identity."

"Believe me Mike I'd love to share your version of events. Regretfully the facts speak for themselves. Personal effects found on the body are conclusive and certain items found inside Granger's flat, plus a positive ID from a close neighbour, all point to one conclusion. Apart from a sister living up in Sheffield, he had no other family. Fortunately we have managed to trace her, and later on she will be in a position to formally identify the body."

"Strangled, I believe you said?"

"Yes, according to the early Path report, that is."

"The poor bastard didn't ask for that, did he? Could it have been a random killing do you think? You know, wrong time, wrong place scenario?"

"Hard to quantify, although the flat itself had been trashed. Clearly the killer was looking for something…money perhaps? Maybe we'll never know."

"And as usual, nobody heard a goddamn thing." Exclaimed Eastern with just a hint of sarcasm.

"If anybody did, then they're keeping it to themselves, although the flat itself is situated in the basement so any unusual noise would have been isolated."

"Motive. What comes to mind?"

"It's too early to speculate Mike. Personally, I wouldn't have thought that he had an enemy in the world, now having met him." Shrugging his shoulders, Rogon issued a token sigh. "And God knows the man had no assets as such." On that assumption, a train of positive thinking channelled Eastern's thoughts.

"I beg to differ Rogon on that one. Assuming that Conway had a case to answer, Granger would have been a prime witness for the prosecution wouldn't he?" Slowly Rogon's late interest began to filter through.

"Correct me if I'm wrong Mike, but are you suggesting Granger's murder was one of convenience? If you're right, then we do have a motive which…"

"If I happened to be a bookie," Eastern interrupted. "I certainly wouldn't want to lay odds against Conway not being involved. The analysis stinks to high hell!"

When expressing his own view, Rogon found himself forced to concur. "When you look at it from that angle, the picture becomes that much clearer. In fact…" he went on. "I'll liaise with Division to lay on a 24/7 update for us to consider. That is, until the initial investigation expires." Equally satisfied that there was nothing more to gain, until specific information become available, the two switched their dual attention into constructing a covert letter. This, in turn, would set out explicit demands in exchange for shared SP. Namely, crucial evidence to support if necessary, a legal claim on the bearer. In this case, a certain Conway senior, alleging his participation in detail consists of acts of conspiracy coinciding with money laundering.

It was also agreed that the said letter would be code signed 'CAGE', that being a euphemism extracted from their joint names. The claim would then be delivered by a courier company of repute, purely to avoid suspicion, and further addressed to a gentleman's club that Conway was known to frequent. Working on the assumption that Conway senior could be guilty as charged, a question of contact came into play.

"This could be a tricky one Mike; we need to contrive a working relationship with the man. But one that can't be traced back to the system. What are your instincts telling you?"

"Nothing really changes Rogon, we are agreed to let Conway do all the running by putting the onus on him. Together we have a set agenda and we need to see it through." Without delving, Eastern sensed a wave of scepticism mounting up in Rogon's direction, at his bluntness.

"Why do I get an impending feeling of one way traffic where your concerned Mike? I can only presume you have something up your sleeve." Grunting, Eastern acknowledged his perception.

"I have as it happens, and, as theories go, I like to think that mine is fool proof... this is what I have in mind." He went on to explain in detail his intended game plan to Rogon.

"Harking on assumption once more, we could include in our letter an added rider that should he request a meet, on the grounds of a financial settlement to relinquish our demands for instance, that he then places an advert in the local 'Argus' newspaper, preferably in the holiday and travel column under the heading:

THE WEATHER IN ROME IS GOOD FOR THIS TIME OF THE YEAR, AND EVEN BETTER ON THE 26/04/2010 AT 3PM UNDER THE CLOCK INSIDE BRIGHTON MAIN LINE TERMINAL

We then sit back and see what happens."

"The station, you don't think it's too open Mike do you? I'm thinking the intervention of Joe Public of course?" queried Rogon.

Confidently putting his mind at rest, Eastern continued where he'd left off: "I've got no qualms about it at all Rogon, surveillance wise, the location in hindsight gives us an edge. Having said that, I wouldn't trust that bastard as far as I could drop him." He paused to allow a dormant thought to surface. "Besides, who's to say he won't use a plant anyway?"

"And if he does, what then?"

"We simply walk away. If we show face, he'll misconstrue it as a form of weakness...it has to be Conway or nothing at all! Let's not forget that we are calling the shots here, and given time it will prove to be his downfall."

"Right! I reckon that just about sums it up then Mike, the 26th you say? That gives us a week to set it all up. I suggest that you take some time out as well in the meantime I'll run our conclusions past the PM's secretary. As for me, I'll continue to remain in touch...oh, there was one other thing."

"Go on." He was hedging.

"The guard they're holding on the Terry Bryant murder. I've been informed that they're getting close to obtaining a full blown confession out of him. If he sings then Conway won't be applying for his pension anyway." There and then their meeting was dissolved, leaving Eastern to his own designs

Arriving back in the village, he didn't hesitate to contact Joan. She assured him that she was fine, and would be staying on in Bloomsbury per se.

Waiting for a kettle to boil over didn't figure in Eastern's make up. Before his head hit the pillow that night, his proactive mind had been alive swirling with plans of his own. Which also included enlisting the aid of DS Curtis.

Chapter Seventeen
A ticket to nowhere

Emerging from out of the shower cubicle, Eastern slipped into a warm towelling robe and made his way into the lounge. Stopping off at the 'mini bar' he busied himself by mixing a drink before making himself comfortable on an adjacent chaise longue. An arm's length away, his leather clad 'bible' sat conveniently on a mall drinks table. Raising his glass in anticipation, he stopped short as the carriage clock on the mantle piece chimed 10am, causing him to grin. "I'll drink to that." He murmured and allowed a wave of satisfaction to wash over his heated frame before stating, "I could well get used to this Rogon. It's called 'getting a life!' but you wouldn't know about that. Would you? Cheers!"

Thirty minutes and an additional Scotch later found him on the second call of the morning. "Johnnie?"

"Hi Mike, good to hear from you, it's been a while. I presume this is a social call?"

"Yes and no mate! The way my life is panning out at the moment it's anything you want it to be. More importantly, how are you coping with the state injected 'holiday'?" It was a throwaway line, forcing Curtis into an induced cough.

"Struggling as well you can imagine Mike, although I still get a cheque paid into my account every week. But you know me mate, I need to get busy. I should have known that the Conway case would have its complications. In retrospect, I should have asked for a posting, but that's easy after the event. How about yourself?"

In spite of their past camaraderie, Eastern reluctantly found himself forced to play down his present spooks image, and return to basics. "I'm still on the case as it were, but nothing too heavy you understand." He then decided, for reasons of his own, to drop the Conway saga completely and move on. "Can I be frank Johnnie? I'm looking for a favour."

"Mike, for fucksake! Where have you been all my life? Just name it. My existence at the moment extends to the nearest shopping mall and back. Right now I couldn't even tell you what I did 10 minutes ago." In ignorance, Curtis had inadvertently played into Eastern's hands simply by misconstruing the word 'favour', to hopefully obtain covert SP relevant to the case. Eastern then made it quite clear as to his intentions, and the reason for his call.

Curtis listened intently as he divulged a coordinated proposal, which would entail an undercover role on his part. As was expected, and bearing in mind his forced exodus, Curtis leapt at the chance to play a significant role alongside Eastern, in what the latter regarded as being a 'personal matter'. In closing, it was made clear that location, times and dates would be verified 24 hours before his services were required.

With the availability of time gifted to him, Eastern felt that the possibility of a clandestine meeting with his nemesis would be counter productive by leaving nothing to chance. Having refuelled his glass and consulted his 'bible', he lost no time in dialling a further beneficial number.

"HQ…Desk Sgt Hayes…can I be of any assistance?"

"I'd like to speak to your DCS Gleason, if it's at all possible?"

"If you can furnish me with your name sir, it may help your cause." Came back the reply.

Eastern bowed to 'jobs worth' and made himself known. A few minutes later and the right connection, the Sgt informed him "You're through Sir." Using Major Travers as a reference, Eastern identified himself by supplying Gleason with an additional code name, enabling him clearance to pursue his intended conversation. Ten or so minutes later, a relieved Eastern was informed that a package containing certain information would be delivered to him later on that day by car.

To the majority of people, the noise of a doorbell sounding off can at times be an irritant. In Eastern's case it became a welcome reprive. Mindful of the fact that he would require a form of ID, he opened his door and found himself confronted by what turned out to be a plain clothed DC, who handed over the desired package. Once indoors, he carefully removed the contents, which revealed a dozen or so photographs, consisting of various mug shots, and an accompanying letter.

Without delving, it quickly became apparent that a percentage of the photos were marked with a distinguishing cross. Having digested the full contents of the package, he printed off a complete new set of the mug shots, and added a directive letter of his own design. Shortly afterwards, a revamped package could be found wending its way via a renowned courier company on to a designer destination.

Relaxing and knowing how to utilise it is one thing, but boredom is as exclusive as can be, leaving Eastern to find out the hard way. Even the chance of taking a flying visit to London for the day out spent with Joan was dashed, purely by spooks dictating events on a daily basis. Finally the breakthrough he'd clamoured for reached boiling point, by emerging five days later, heralded by the hyped up voice of Rogon breaking the stalemate.

"Yeah, it's good news Mike, we have had a response at last so now we have to assume that Conway has taken the bait." He went on to state that their proposed reply featured in the latest edition of the 'Argus'. As a result, a car would be made available in an hour's time to fetch him in for a detailed briefing and seal their intended plans on operation code named 'CAGE'. A few hours later, a deflated Rogon expressed his own personal views on the outcome of their discussion. "I guess that just about sums it all up Mike. I'm pretty confident that we haven't missed anything out, but if I have, now is the time to speak."

"That won't be necessary Rogon, knowing that our house is in full order, the outcome rests solely in Conway's corner." The meeting was then adjourned per se, after further agreeing that Eastern would be acting as the decoy spokesman on the day. On the return journey back to the village, Eastern had a change of heart and asked to be dropped off in the vicinity of his old flat. Apart from the ongoing smell arising from the existing dampness, and the token grief from a door lock that had a life of its own, nothing it seemed, had really changed.

His intentions once inside the bed sit were pre planned as he went about his routine in a business like manner. Disconnecting his landline, he rummaged through a mountain of personal demands and junk mail purely out of habit. Minutes later, and satisfied there was nothing to be gained for his trouble, he opened a small concealed wall safe and removed a cloth covered item. It was then slipped reverently inside his coat pocket. Seemingly at ease with himself, he gave a last lingering glance around the room. Turning the key in the lock, he left and made his way downstairs. Once outside, he shuddered involuntarily as a blast of cold air caught him out. Immediately opposite, the captivating odour of cooking issuing from the 'OVERDONE RASHER' wafted across the street, prompting him into making a snap decision.

"Yeah, why not? It's been a while, besides I could use a coffee." The unmistakeable tones of the proprietor Benny Weismann, greeted him as he entered the café.

"Hi Mike! It's nice to see you…you're getting to be a stranger already."

Ordering a coffee, Eastern let it be known that he'd been currently involved on a case which entailed working out of town, hence the lapse in custom. Eastern's spontaneous appearance had now struck a memory nerve with Benny, making him eager to offload a pent up mystery. "…and so by now Mike, I'm thinking to myself, things ain't kosher. In fact, that's the second time this week that the 'face' comes in demanding questions about you. But don't you worry my boy I always keep schtum. Besides, the 'shmuck' never spent a coin."

A recipe of concern added to a sudden adrenalin rush are not compatible with hot coffee it seems. Pushing his cup to one side, Eastern invited Weismann to describe the stranger to him as best he could. The most prominent observation being a scar above the left eye. Satisfied with the play back, Eastern was quick to extend his gratitude. "Thanks for the SP Benny, I owe you one. Knowing what I know now

I'll take a rain check on the coffee if you don't mind." Throwing a £10 note on the counter, he exclaimed "I'll be in touch." Turning on his heel, he left like a man bent on a mission.

Five minutes later having secured a cab, he found himself back inside his flat poring over the mug shots that he'd previously copied. Moments later his body stiffened as one face in particular seemed to reach out and grab his attention. The knowing look engrained on his face spoke volumes. "Well, well. You're even uglier than Rogon is, you sad bastard!" He said with conviction. "Now let's see what your CV has to say, ah here we are. Lenny Robbins, age 39, career criminal...dozen or so convictions ranging from GBH to a get away driver." The last reference caused him to start, as a past altercation came back to haunt him. "Yeah, it all fits. I reckon we've met before Mr Fucking Robbins, although the next time will be on my terms."

"Cometh the hour, cometh the man," That is, if fate is led to be believed. In this particular case, the 'man' just happened to be assistant Chief Constable Conway. With less than 24 hours left to go prior to their alleged meet coming to fruition, Mike Eastern was fronting a tight rope schedule based on a war of nerves. "I wouldn't want it any other way." He would insist if challenged. "Not only that, but it gives a man an edge, and that's the key." He'd been expecting it for some time now so he wasn't unduly concerned when the phone finally kicked off. It also reminded him that he had two calls of his own to pursue.

"Rogon! What took you so long?"

"You can blame Division for that Mike, but I can assure you that the wait is well worth it." Temporarily, Eastern's mind could be found lodged elsewhere, and it didn't include a third party presence.

"Division? We've got our own damn agenda, I don't..." Rogon was forced to intervene and quickly dispelled any outside interest.

"It's our show and always has been, the reason I'm calling is there's been a major breakthrough in locating the owner of the PIB. All thanks to Division, I have to say. Apparently, Reggie Greenford, as he was known, sold up some years ago and moved to Spain. In fact, shortly after the reign of protection racket existed."

"Are you now telling me that they've managed to track him down?"

A short lull followed, implying to Eastern that Rogon could be hedging on something."

"It would appear." He went on, "That our less than explicit editor was killed in a 'sensitive' hit and run accident 12 months after settling in. To make matters worse, the report stated that it was dark at the time and even worse that there were no witnesses. I'll leave you to form your own conclusions on that score. Incidentally, he was succeeded by a daughter who is currently residing in Essex and, so I'm told, currently available for questioning for what it's worth."

"Was there any motive attached to his death at the time?"

"Not as such, although the Spanish police at one point suggested that blackmail could have been behind it. On investigation, Greenford's bank account it seems went up and down like a flaming yoyo."

"Shit! It doesn't get any better does it?" Eastern sounded off. "Conway's even left a stink in Europe by the sound of it. That's what comes of having the benefit of an offshore account. Somebody had a nice 'sweetener' and bloody untraceable in the bargain." With priorities at the heart of the matter, Rogon had ensured that everything was in place from his end for the following day, since having top level clearance to proceed with their join enterprise.

Surprisingly enough, Eastern rejected a late offer to be 'hot wired' in the knowledge that Conway's position and experience could, for some reasons unknown, possibly work against him. Having said that, he did leave Rogon with a later poser to grapple with, by admitting "I'll be using a few ideas of my own on the day."

That evening, after showering, a subdued and mentally tired Eastern decided that cooking for one was a non starter and eventually settled for a curry takeaway and the promise of an early night.

Just before retiring, he dealt with two outstanding calls. The first of which was brief to say the least, and apart from hello and goodbye, consisted of four words but each riddled with anticipation. The first call stated that 'Rome is definitely burning." The second call entailed a lengthy conversation with Joan, and finished on a high note. Not long after, any doubts he may have harboured as regards a sleepless night suitably vanished as his head collided with the pillow.

They say 'they' being the operative word and for the majority of this case is that your initial instinct is generally the right one, and yet with pompous disregard, nobody had bothered to question his views on the subject - based purely on his exclusive maverick style when confronted with an explosive issue. The moment that he awoke the following morning, he felt an impending sense of foreboding. Without hesitation, the negative thought became a distant statistic. As he summed up its departure later, "To hell with it, don't they know that I get off on that line of thinking?" would be his answer to all of his critics. "Besides, a problem only becomes a problem when you exasperate it. Personally, I much prefer the word challenge." So here endeth the first lesson according to Mike Eastern.

That apart, there was no way he could have forecast how many 'lessons' he would need to confront that same day as minute by minute, the huge central clock inside Brighton Station ticked mercilessly away, bent on an exclusive countdown, before climaxing into a pre-arranged meet between himself and his decadent nemesis Conway Senior. With less than an hour to go, Eastern's mind and body leapfrogged from a sense of normality into one of reality. At least he was now reassigned to whatever lay in store and in the process, leaving Rogon as a mere spectator for once. Although in hindsight he did carry one nagging thought that in spite of his singular commitment, the latter would never stray far from the perimeter of a situation.

Alighting from the bus outside the station became the easy part. In contrast the minute he entered the main terminal, a massive surge of adrenalin boosted a natural flow of expectancy. Basic instincts then took over, as he decided to head for a mobile refreshment stand, suitably adjacent to the central clock. In spite of having the percentage advantage of cover, he sensed a feeling that a thousand pairs of eyes were boring directly into his back.

Aware that it was only still 2.45pm, he noted that the main terminal was exceptionally busy for the time of day. Not that it was of any consequence on his part. The only interest surrounding him lay in the path of one person. He felt his throat tighten up in anticipation causing his mouth to run dry. With time on his hands, he ordered a coffee before deciding to make his first move. Although his vantage point allowed him the benefit of a clear view, it was only made possible when a break occurred due to the thronging crowds of would be commuters. In the event there was no evidence to suggest that as yet, his covert offer had been taken seriously.

At least he had the added advantage of recognition, should Conway decide to play ball, by having first hand knowledge of the man overall. As opposed to the latter attempting to do business with a complete and utter stranger...or so he thought! Minutes later Eastern's body stiffened and he appeared to be distracted. Slowly lowering his coffee cup, he allowed the corners of his mouth to twitch into the first phase of a smile, tinged with relief. No! He hadn't made a mistake, although it took a double take to satisfy himself. He could just make out the figure of a man, notably holding a newspaper under his arm, while standing directly underneath the shadow of the clock.

"Could well be I'm in business at last," was his initial feeling. Discarding his coffee, he took a leisurely stroll toward the lone figure. In no time at all, he realised that his assumption regarding Conway's participation was now flawed, owing to the fact that the alleged stranger was none other than the getaway driver who'd previously made an unsuccessful attempt to run him down. Luckily for Eastern, the only eye contact between the two had been made on his own behalf. Forcing himself to make a snap decision, his reaction was short and swift, turning on his heel he strode away from the scene to regain his composure, at the same time grabbing himself some all important thinking time.

According to the clock, he only had three minutes left, in which to form a genuine conclusion. With so many possible scenarios flying around in his head at one time, his pumped up brain needed to click into overtime. Foremost on his mind would be to make a decision based on contact. The chances being, that the situation could well formulate into a catch 22 situation. In so much as he would be damned into fulfilling the meet with the obvious decoy and therefore literally blowing his cover. Or, at worst, damned if he reneged on the deal anyway, fearing that it would show a sign of weakness on his part.

"Fucksake! It was never intended to turn out this way!" He cursed, and rebuked himself for undermining Conway's art of deception by backing him into a corner and forcing him to put his neck on the line.

In the end, it was a case of put up or shut up, as Eastern suddenly halted in his tracks. "I've never yet walked away from a situation that spelled grief." He told himself through gritted teeth. "And I don't intend to start now!" This was now Eastern at his best by wallowing in a scenario he felt comfortable in. Any paid up shares he may have invested with sensibility in mind, became instantly devalued.

Grim faced, he turned on his heel and headed for the clock, while facing the prospect of an unconventional date with a decoy. At the very last moment, he veered off course, deciding that he'd approach Conway's whipping boy from behind, to gain an element of surprise. Given the situation, you could almost excuse Eastern for his well mannered diplomacy as he tapped the figure on the shoulder. "Excuse me...were you expecting to meet somebody here?" He enquired. Completely caught off balance, the man swung round to confront him. A look of utter disbelief etched his face as recognition set in. As auditions go, his effort was deemed to be brief as the exist doors closed tight behind him.

"You?...you...but!"

Capitalising on his strategic move, Eastern was swift to put him out of his misery. "Yeah, guess who? You arsehole. I'm the last person you expected to see, not that it'll do you any favours of course. You're getting a bit of a bad habit fucking things up just lately." Leaning forward Eastern then spoke low and meaningfully into the traumatised man's ear. "I happen to know that you're on Conway's payroll, which makes you a long time loser. You should know that the guy doesn't give a toss what happens to you. For once in your shit life do the right thing and expose the arrogant bastard for what he is. Whatever way you look at it, I think you need to brush up on your dominoes. I'm told that Bellmarsh are looking for new members at the moment...know what I mean?"

Pent up retaliation then broke surface, leaving his aggressor to reply with a verbal backlash of his own. "You're all mouth Eastern." The man retorted. "I should have taken you out the last time we met. You haven't got a clue as to what's going down and who you're dealing with. You're way out of your league. Take my advice, do yourself a favour by walking away while you're still breathing." The last thing he wanted at this stage was to make a scene, and Eastern was aware that their confrontation was beginning to get heated. Foremost on his mind meant cutting his losses by forcing a closure of some kind. Unfortunately, the hood had unexpected ideas of a rather more drastic scenario.

Without any warning, the sudden sensation emerging from the snub end of a revolver made contact with his ribcage causing him to gasp. "I should have known better you fucking freak. The newspaper! You obviously didn't buy it to read. I presume there's a shooter hidden in there."

"You'd better start believing it Eastern, and I'm well paid for using it. From now on, you do as I say, got it?" Convinced that his oppressor meant business, and the chance that the public might be exposed to danger left Eastern with no choice but to go along with his demands. Just then, his gaze was averted as he glanced over the hood's shoulder. He made out the sight of a man in full flight, weaving his way through a horde of people in his direction, intent on catching a belated train or so Eastern imagined. At the last moment, the impulsive commuter veered directly into the gunman's side, catching him totally unawares. The sudden impact in turn, jolted the firearm from his possession, and left it spinning harmlessly on the ground. Eastern immediately kicked the offending weapon safely to one side. With no fight left in him, the hood offered little resistance making it easy for Eastern to overpower him. Meanwhile, the alleged commuter recovered the firearm by way of a handkerchief and turned to confront a much relieved Eastern. From the off, it became obvious that the two shared more than a chance meeting. "Thanks Johnnie, I was beginning to wonder where the hell you had got to. Mind you, you're timing wasn't all that bad mate. I owe you one."

"I'll keep you to that, Mike." DS Curtis replied emphatically. "But you did say to keep a low profile as I recall. It was only when I spotted the newspaper that I realised the arsehole couldn't have been a crossword fan…know what I mean?"

"Yeah right, never off the case eh? Listen, you'd better get on your toes, the railway plod are on their way over…I'll contact you tonight and thanks again."

The best part of an hour later, was spent recycling police protocol at Division. Soon after, Eastern took advantage of a lift home with Traffic patrol. Minutes before climbing into the squad car, the sudden appearance of CS Gleason venturing across to him later gave rise to mutual concern. Gleason was clearly rehearsed on Eastern's presence, by leaving a nasty little taste in his mouth when expressing his views on the outcome of the station incident per se. It wasn't what he suggested but the manner in which it were implied that ignited a dormant cell of doubt to reappear should the man's integrity come under scrutiny.

"Eastern! You're getting to be a bad habit just lately. They tell me that this latest involvement is the second life threatening assault in as many weeks." Pausing for a brief moment as if to select his words in summing up, he continued in a sardonic manner. "It makes me wonder just how lucky can a man get, considering the facts. I would need to take heed if it was me, should a third attempt rise."

Eastern was nobody's fool, and prided himself on his perceptivity. This had now left him convinced, that their spontaneous conversation was far from being kosher. On the journey back to the village, his congested mind became reluctant to let the matter drop. Once indoors and with the uplifting benefit from his first Scotch of the day, he allowed his recharged brain to trigger off a series of alarming facts consistent with the car park incident at Division. "Fact one, how would the driver of the vehicle have possibly known that I was going to be there at that time? Fact two, he would have needed to have been aware prior to my arrival and likely directed from a third party source. Fact three, the only person who could have known my movements had to be CS Gleason, whom I'd spent a good hour with when discussing certain aspects of the case."

Based on a whim and a reference, (he reminded himself of the past conversation that he'd had with Joan's step father), in his eyes Gleason came across as being untouchable and a credit to the uniform. Conclusion: "If my judgement holds any substance, I could well be forced into asking myself that just maybe, the person who has remained our enigma for so long, our 'Mr Big' has been genuinely lurking in the background all this time, and myself and others haven't been aware."

For his part Eastern wasn't buying Major Travers' version,

experience had taught him otherwise. And on balance, when provided with the facts, like it or not Gleason's involvement in a would be conspiracy held water. His case only got better with each mouthful of Scotch, as he surveyed the theory of a Conway and Gleason double act. "At least now I've got something of interest to throw at Rogon when I phone him later to explain how the meet panned out."

If, as they say, 'news travels fast' then Rogon must have been sitting in the next room exploring his comments. Minutes later and full of expectancy, he gently lifted the phone. All bets were void as the cutting tones of Rogon claimed his air space. "Before you attempt to explain away, what could have resulted in a major situation with far reaching consequences..." Eastern had heard and experienced more than enough for one day. Right now he didn't relish a verbal confrontation, especially coming from a plastic so called colleague.

"Rogon, shut it! I can well do without your verbal crap. Now you damn well listen to me you fucking moron. I don't recall anything in my brief mentioning a vicar's tea party. As far as I'm concerned, we had a result today. Not only is there one less arsehole on the street but I've also come up with a new theory, conducive to the case that could prove to be gilt edged. The evidence alone is admissible, I suspect that the IPCC will have a field day on the strength of it."

"Really? My apologies, I guess I was a touch too judgemental, your latest theory sounds promising. I'll order a car..."

"Not today you won't Rogon." Eastern snapped. "The rest of the day belongs to me. Whatever I've got to say is going to have to wait until tomorrow morning. Sometimes you seem to forget I've also got a life, and right now it's outside of the agency." Smugness! Or just plain downright resolute? His delivery method wouldn't have wavered either way. The sheer satisfaction in knowing that Rogon had completely absorbed his latest theory had been compensation enough.

The evening was still young enough to enable him to occupy himself with his own devices. First consideration on his agenda lay with DS Curtis, by extending his gratitude for his timely intervention earlier on in the day. Eastern brought him up to speed on the events following his assailant's arrest, and the likelihood that Conway Senior could possibly amount to being the 'tip of the iceberg' as conspirators go. In closing, Curtis made his position clear should his assistance remain an option, in spite of being in limbo.

The flip side to most theories is that they do tend to blow up in your face, occasionally due to an over active brain. There's always that nagging reminder that just maybe you could be wrong. Right now Eastern's head began to resemble the likes of a punch bag, and with every scenario surfacing, the pain just seemed to get worse. "For Christ's sake!" he exclaimed in frustration, "I'm letting the poxy case get to me. I need something more solid to wrestle with. Of course! Why the hell didn't I think of that before?" Downing his Scotch, he grabbed his mobile and hastily dialled an out of city number from memory. Seconds later he made the connection.

"Travers residence, lady of the house speaking. How may I help?"

"I apologise for phoning you at this hour, but please could you inform the Major, that Mike Eastern would like a word, thank you. Oh, and it's rather important." He added.

"Hold the line, Mike, I do so hope it isn't a problem, I'll put you through to the study." Came back the reply. Moments later, the unmistakeable tones of Major Travers honed in.

"Hello dear boy. What appears to be the trouble? Celia suggested there might be a problem." Eastern then went on to emphasise that his call was of a delicate matter the backbone of which entailed personal information regarding DCS Gleason's background. At this stage, he elected to keep his single minded theory under wraps to avoid the possibility that his enquiry could lead to a misrepresentation of personalities. A foreboding silence ensued as Travers digested the facts.

"That's rather a tough one old chap, code of ethics and all that... what! Mind you, I presume your motive for asking has to have a bearing on your current investigation. Having said that, I feel that we can find some middle ground here." Eastern then attempted to further his knowledge over and above what he already knew about Gleason which included a much sought after opinion on the latter's relationship with his acting superior, assistant Police Constable Conway. It wasn't long before a mental picture began to evolve in his mind, as certain impromptu facts began to emerge.

High on the list concerned a little friendship between the two, stemming back to their public school days together, followed by a dual military association. In conclusion, the Major also let it be known that their social lives extended to sharing a membership at a particular private members club, "Situated in Hove don't you know?"

It was a jubilant Eastern that recharged his glass following the call. Based on the fact that he was already aware of the club's existence, an idea began to form in his mind. The difference being that this time around the outcome would rest solely with himself.

The next morning, a regenerated Eastern drove to the Brighton office, owned by Inner City Courier Services Ltd who'd previously dealt with the conveyance of his own original blackmail letter. With the aid of his exclusive ID he made himself known, and asked to see a copy of the original delivery note, that accompanied the package left in their charge. Scrutinising the form only got better. The two signatures featured on the receipt, one signed the other printed, would be priceless as future admissible evidence. "I'll be taking this document along with me, so I advise you make a copy for your own files." He explained to the manager, "And should he be on the premises, I'd like a word with the courier who delivered it." Once the driver appeared, Eastern produced a head and shoulders copy of a figure taken from a photograph and confronted him with it. "Do you happen to recognise this person at all?" He enquired. "Take your time, it happens to be important you understand."

The driver's reaction to his request only confirmed his suspicions, that the blackmail letter had been conveniently secreted thus leaving Conway oblivious to its contents.

"Sure, I wouldn't forget that face in a hurry!" he exploded. "Right bumptious type as a I recall. I remember asking him if he could locate the person who's name was on the package and he said he's not available at the moment, but I'll sign for it and make sure he gets it. I only needed a signature as proof of delivery so it didn't make any difference to me. Not only that!" he emphasised, "The tight bastard didn't even tip me." Eastern thanked him and nodded sympathetically.

"There was one other thing. Your delivery procedure, how does it work?"

"I simply carry a clipboard containing a biro on a chain, and hand it over to the customer to endorse the delivery note."

"I see. So he would have to hold the clipboard while he signed them?"

"Absolutely, like I said." With visions of forensics in his mind, Eastern had nothing to lose and made it clear he would need to remove the clipboard for detailed examination. He thanked the manager once again and made his way back to the village. For the second time in as many minutes, his mobile reminded him that Rogon was never off the case. Chuckling to himself, he continued to let it ring on a premise that it would finally piss him off. But once indoors, there was no escape, not that he was concerned. His day had started well, and he had every intention in making sure it stayed that way.

Chapter Eighteen
The beginning of the end

Eastern had good cause to feel uneasy. The bland expression on Rogon's face began to radiate a form of negativity. He should have guessed that his luck only lay in one direction, with an added time limit attached. An hour or so earlier he had been feeling on top of his game, but he hadn't reckoned on the intervention issuing from a timely bout of cynicism aimed in his direction.

"No! I'm sorry Mike, there's too much at stake here, it just won't wash. You could have got yourself killed yesterday. Therefore I can't see the powers that be sanctioning your proposal. You tend to forget that I have to answer to a higher authority."

"Yeah, so you keep reminding me. He's probably an ex member of the pin stripe suit and bowler hat brigade, who spends 90% of his life fast asleep in the Lords and, when it comes to grass root policing, you can bet he doesn't know shit from shit! Okay, maybe I do take the odd risk to obtain a result, but heads I win, tails I don't works for me."

Rogon winced at his homespun honesty and centred on the alleged evidence put forward by Eastern.

"I have to say Mike, that in my opinion this fresh evidence that you've collated is very subjective, even assuming of course, that forensic can come up with a genuine finger print. The two signatures alone aren't enough to prove that Gleason intercepted our package, anybody could have copied them. At the very least we would require a specimen of handwriting to authenticate them."

Eastern felt a sudden upturn in Rogon's temperament at what he considered to be delaying tactics. "What fucking planet are you on for Christ's sake? I've told you I've got a witness standing by who…"

"Doesn't know Gleason from Father Christmas?" Rogon inferred vehemently. "Without a print we are stymied, like it or not the two have to match. In the meantime, I suggest we work on a fresh approach and give forensic the hurry up." Eastern then let it be known that he wanted more from his current input by offering a ready made solution.

"I want a plant on the inside." He suggested. "I've been thinking, would we gain anything by using a mole working under cover in the club that they frequent?"

"I accept that your idea is worthy of consideration Mike. Leave that one with me, I need to dwell on it. By the way, the security guard in the Bryant case is due to come up for trial next week, that'll be interesting in itself."

"Really, although you never did say?"

"Say? About what?"

"The clemency deal on offer, did you ever reinstate it?" Rogon shrugged his shoulders in a care free manner. At the same time, a token mask of disappointment crossed his face.

"Strangely enough we did, having said that, the stupid bastard turned it down at the eleventh hour. However, if we can get a fix on Gleason, there's a damn good chance he could renege and settle for the same deal."

"Huh, that only gives us a week. I still say that we force the issue and confront Gleason and worry about the damage afterward."

"I admire your tenacity Mike, you've got more front than Russia I'll give you that. Quietly laughing to himself, Rogon continued: "Which reminds me, I need to contact Division this morning to see if they have made any headway with your gunman friend." Returning the humour, Eastern smiled in his own exclusive fashion.

"Give me an empty cell and five minutes and I'll hand you his bleedin' life story." In spite of his 'plastic shell' Rogon was forced to briefly admit that Eastern's attitude, given the circumstances, did carry a significant purpose to it. Diplomacy then swiftly converted his alien thoughts back to reality.

"Always the maverick, aren't you Mike? Believe it or not I'm going to miss you when this is all over." If anybody had handed him a winning lottery ticket, the look on Eastern's face would have had the same effect at Rogon's spontaneous disclosure.

For a second he was stunned before firing back: "And here's me thinking that spooks have a metal input tray instead of a heart. You certainly had me fooled for a minute."

"On the contrary Mike, although we do share one common factor... justice!"

On the return journey back home, he asked to be dropped off at a convenience store with the intention of grabbing a few groceries. Moments later, any suggestion that the shopping held importance became quietly shattered when the midday edition of the 'Argus' drew his attention toward the stop press.

ASSISTANT POLICE CONSTABLE SHOCK REVELATION
A spokesperson representing the IPCC, investigating the ongoing DCI Conway conspiracy, have released a report this morning stating that Conway Senior has been officially suspended from duty forthwith, while their case continues. The spokesperson has also denied any reports that their decision has implicated him in any way, and that it was purely a matter of routine.

His first initial reaction was to contact Rogon, but he decided that there was nothing to gain by this action, and that Rogon in all probability had been made aware anyway. Drawing on to his own conclusion to the article, it soon became evident that Conway Senior's role, if any in the conspiracy, was now showing signs of open vindication, bearing in mind the intensity of the operation. At the same time, the case for Gleason in his opinion had now strengthened, by leaving him as the front runner to take over the prime mantel of chief suspect.

Left with time on his hands, a restless Eastern decided that he needed to catch up with Joan. Acting on advice, and based on the fact that her estranged husband had yet to take the stand, she wisely elected to keep out of the limelight and reconciled herself into staying with her journalist friend in Bloomsbury throughout the whole trial.

"You have to say that the climate isn't looking good for Conway, considering the build up of uneasy facts in the past, wouldn't you say?" Expressing his views via a personalised phone link to Rogon the next day, Eastern was keen to hear the latter's views regarding the latest press coverage. In hindsight, he wished that he hadn't bothered as the line appeared to be dead. "Rogon! Hello, are you still there?" There didn't seem to be any response whatsoever. He was also aware that his timing could have been that much better. In no time at all it became clear that once their conversation resumed, it was liable to be more than just a routine follow up.

As he suspected, his perception held water. As for Rogon, he allowed his customary philosophical manner to set a precedent, "It's far too early for me to comment at this stage Mike, although on reflection, our timing was right to have a change of direction, and at the same time concentrate our efforts entirely on Gleason."

"And what about the IPCC, don't they have a say in the matter?" Eastern snapped back with a hint of sarcasm.

"Without having to castigate, let's just say we helped them make their mind up into having a review on strategy." Talk and more talk equals frustration, and Eastern wasn't in the mood for mind games.

"That's total bollocks Rogon, I should imagine that they were the last to know the situation. So bloody level with me and give me a straight answer." Which begs the question, how does anybody hide a smile within a smile? In his case, albeit a spook he would have been hard pressed to conceive the drawback one way or another, unless of course that person had privy to a form of back up. Simple enough question, but coming from Eastern one that was worth studying to capitalise on. "Well? That knowing look will do for a start, all you need to do is to elaborate on the truth of the matter?"

"In that case, I take it that you'll be pleased to know that we made a breakthrough at last. The lab boys have obtained a DNA match taken from the courier's clipboard coinciding with the delivery note. So, on the strength of that I'd have to say that your hunch regarding our friend Gleason, was a good call on your part Mike." As good as the newfound evidence projected, it still left Eastern facing an unfinished problem.

"Well on that score, it more than proves that Gleason deliberately set me up at Brighton railway station. Although what we don't know for certain is whether or not he passed our blackmail letter on to Conway. The flip side being, that the two could well be collaborating as an item."

"Point taken Mike. Unfortunately, the gunman himself is holding the answer to that one we fear. So Division are going to work much harder on him. Failing that, there are other options at our disposal we can call on."

"Yeah right! And in the meantime, we're left playing the waiting game once more. What the hell are you waiting for? You've got enough SP on Gleason at this moment in time to charge him on two counts of conspiracy to murder, full stop!"

You're right of course Mike, the guy has had a good run, so we need to take the initiative while the iron's hot. Not only that, it's bound to keep the PM off my back. I'll contact the IPCC meanwhile and arrange a meeting. They can use the evidence we have amassed and go from there. The sooner the Home Office can issue a warrant then so much the better."

"Fucking Amen to that." Eastern sanctioned and then added, "My only regret is that I won't be present when they read the bastard his rights."

"I wouldn't dwell on that Mike, although satisfaction is a great leveller. Incidentally I received a memo from Division yesterday that slipped my mind."

"It's obviously not that important."

"That remains to be seen Mike, the memo itself refers to the late Paul Granger. Can you ever recall him mentioning the fact that he'd considered contacting Division prior to knowing you?"

Eastern shook his head vigorously, "Absolutely no way Rogon, I'd have remembered something that critical. Anyway, what would his reasons have been for doing so?"

"Just that it ties in with the speculation that initially emerged from the tabloids regarding Conway's alleged role in the conspiracy. In fact, Granger made a sworn statement if you recall, stating that he had circumstantial evidence which if proven could damage Conway's case..." He was cut short by Eastern's swift intervention.

"Namely the PIB that he was in possession of at that time. The poor guy virtually planned his own death warrant by walking into a trap of his own design. There was no way that he could have known that Gleason was also bent. And the outcome that ensued, whoever killed Granger, desperately wanted that PIB and was willing enough to commit murder to get it. The only consolation being the fact that we are now in possession of it and this has rebounded on Gleason...that's what I call KARMA." The cynical smile that he then evoked summed up his inner feelings. "His death was collateral damage at its worst. If only he'd confided in me, there's a chance he could be alive today."

Nodding briskly, Rogon was quick to concur, "Unfortunately Mike, life is cheap, but in Gleason's case his involvement in bringing it about will prove costly."

Later on that evening as predicted, a team led by the representative of the IPCC duly charged Gleason on various accounts of conspiracy and murder. A laptop along with boxes of personal files and effects were also removed from his residence. Once in custody, Gleason found himself subjected to an intense programme of questioning. Needless to say, he was eager to cooperate, with whatever was thrown at him, including his alleged role in the murder of DC Bryant. As one particular interrogator put it, "It was almost as if he couldn't wait to bring the whole damn rotten mess out into the open. I could see an unmistakeable look of relief in the man's eyes as he opened up."

When questioned about his alleged association with the two Conways he was clearly explicit, almost to the letter. "The assistant Chief Constable, to my knowledge, had not knowingly participated in any of the conspiracies I am being charged with." Leading on from that, he was also quick to exonerate Conway junior of the murder. "Who," he stated, "Was completely oblivious of my intention to dispose of Bryant. It became a moment of utter madness on my part. He was the one person who could have exposed the ongoing corruption that existed. Once you had arrested DCI Conway, I sensed that everything was closing in around me. I realised then that I had to remove Bryant from the equation. Unfortunately for him, his untimely death became possible with the collaboration of the in house security guard, whom you're holding in custody as we speak."

When asked to make a separate statement regarding his involvement in the life threatening incidents on Eastern's life, he seemed reluctant to go into detail, simply stating: "The evidence you have is pretty conclusive in itself, wouldn't you say? Your Mr Eastern, or whoever he is, became an enigma to say the least. And, as such, I underestimated his sheer tenacity. It's fair to say that he brought about the beginning of the end, as far as I'm concerned."

Later he went on record by declaring: "As I recall, the initial case that kick started the conspiracy right up to its present level, came into being some years ago." Pausing briefly, a look of mixed emotions swept through his racked body, causing him to shudder as a sudden pang of guilt buried itself deep inside his brain, at the same time seeking a form of resurrection. "The Dowling case...I remember it now...it's all coming back to me. I never realised how easy it became to look the other way. That is, until the bung syndrome came into play. Once I'd dealt with any misgivings the situation quickly blossomed into a habit flushed with greed. It was almost too easy at times, due to the system we imposed. I would like to impress that on reflection, Dowling was no more guilty of Spelling's murder than the judge at his trial. The man never stood a chance with his previous. It only aided to ensure that our blatant cover up was sustainable. I can even give you the name of the true murderer. As for the bung, all monies were secreted via an offshore account. From then on, the harvest only got better as between us we reaped the rewards. That is, until the spooks got involved. From then on, it was just a matter of time before we were exposed."

At that point, and the fact that he was obviously racked with guilt, prompted the interrogating officer to ask Gleason for his views on the two other officers already facing trial for their role in the conspiracy. Declining the offer, Gleason simply stated the real truth will emerge one way or another. Having said that, it takes a man to operate a car before it can be of any use!" The off the cuff remark was sidelined at the time in favour of, "He's lost the plot, and finally peaked."

The following morning while still in custody, the duty watch Sgt discovered Gleason's lifeless body lying on his bed. Protruding from his mouth, the short end of a sock was clearly visible. To all intents and purposes, he had attempted to choke himself to death, and in doing so induced a massive heart attack. It didn't take long before spooks headed by Rogon became privy to certain information.

"Mike! Apologies if I've got you out of bed, but apparently there's a situation over at Division. And I respectfully think you ought to be aware of it before it hits the media circus."

"Calm down Rogon, it's not even 8 o clock yet. Fucksake, have a day off, I'm sure Division can handle whatever grief it is without my assistance?" Knowing Eastern as well as he did meant that there was only one approach left to him.

"Gleason! Gleason is dead!" First hand shock, especially the spontaneous type can become a personal outlet to the body when it's delivered, although the present time of day could have some bearing on its outcome.

"Rogon, don't mess with me, it's too early for whatever you've got in mind. Just say whatever you've got to say and leave it at that!" Any recrimination on his part went clean over his head, leaving Rogon to carry on their conversation where he'd left off.

"From what I've been told Mike, he committed suicide in the early hours of this morning according to the latest path report. There will of course be a post mortem, but I can safely say that my account is pretty conclusive. You were due to come in this morning anyway for a debrief but Gleason's untimely death changes everything. I'll get some transport laid on for you at around 9.30am…until then Mike." He then hung up, leaving one totally shocked Eastern wishing he'd never picked the phone up.

"It's only just beginning to get through to me. Although when you consider what the man would be facing, it as probably the best thing he could have done given the circumstances. At worse he's saved the state a nice few quid."

Seated around a table at spooks HQ with Rogon as a companion resulted in the second shock to his system that morning. With the state coffee coming a tight third...It was soon left to Rogon to set the wheels in motion, and the possibility of another.

"You didn't really know Gleason that well did you Mike? Outside of work that is?"

"No! Not at all, although Major Travers, who was his superior up until he retired, put him on a pedestal. He also mentioned the fact that Conway senior and Gleason were joined at the hip going back as far as public school days. Oh, and he wasn't married either, but that was public knowledge anyway. Why do you ask?"

"Uhm, no particular reason Mike, except to say that my take on the association differs somewhat from yours."

"Strange, I can't see how Rogon. What I've just told you was related to me in confidence. In fact, Travers also stated that the two actually shared military ties as well at one stage." It soon became evident by his body language that Rogon, for some reason or another, could be seen to be looking uncomfortable with Eastern's findings, and even more so because of their origin. For the time being, any further thoughts on the subject were put to one side as Rogon prepared himself for another fresh stance.

"You've got a busy day ahead of you I'm afraid Mike. I have the transcripts taken from the statements made by Gleason. I want you to delve through the wording to ensure that nothing has been left out." Eastern's face dropped, as he angrily turned to face Rogon.

"You just don't get it do you? It's over...finished, the whole bloody case is wrapped up, and you've achieved the result that you set out for. Think about it? The PM is now going to get his sleep at night, while 'Mr Big' is lying stone cold on a slab in the path lab counting bleedin' sheep 24/7...I mean c'mon." Undaunted by Eastern's verbal assassination, he promptly allowed his outburst to fly gracefully over his head, and continued where he left off.

"I don't have to stress the importance of what I'm asking you to do Mike. If there is anything untoward in his existence, you are the only man I know who could possibly unearth it. So I take it that's a yes then?" Eastern should have read the signs, but when you're dealing with plastic as opposed to flesh and bone, it made the term ambiguous totally redundant.

"Anybody else but you Rogon." He sighed deeply, what am I looking for in particular?"

"For once you have got carte blanche on an open mind Mike and that's why I have requested you to do it…and good luck." Left to his own devices, Eastern surveyed the paperwork lying on the desk in front of him. They seemed to mock his presence, causing him to mutter in a languid manner.

"Well! Thanks but no thanks Rogon." A secondary thought then escaped him. "At least I know what I'll be doing for the rest of the day…alone!" Armed with a pen and note pad, he then proceeded to unravel as to what lay in the transcripts. A few mentally strained hours later, Rogon made himself known. In the one hand he could be seen to be clutching an A4 type buff envelope.

Eastern glanced upwards and quipped: "Hum, I see you've brought me some wages then?"

Rogon's facial expression remained motionless as he replied in a cynical manner. "When you have a minute, I need you to examine some photographs which you will find in this envelope." Placing the package down, he continued to speak in his own exclusive and robotic manner. "A word of advice Mike, don't look for the obvious, you could be mistaken for taking them at face value." Eastern was forced to chuckle at his double edged request and fired back.

"You're talking in riddles again Rogon, but I take your point."

An unmoved Rogon then put a cap on their brief conversation. "You can forget any qualms I may have held in that direction. I feel assured that your views on the subject will be highly interesting." Turning on his heel, he left the office leaving a befuddled Eastern to adjust his thoughts.

"Patronising sod." He told himself. "But I suppose as spooks go, he's not all that bad."

Some hours later, and surrounded by a dozen or so empty cups of stale coffee, he stretched his back and eased himself back into his chair and reflected on his input. "Bearing in mind the original conversation that we had, I can see now where Rogon was coming from regarding the

The beginning of the end

photos. As for the transcripts, I could visualise a code cracker having a field day examining them." He openly remarked in a buoyant fashion.

Pressing a nearby button, he requested that Rogon makes an appearance. Minutes later, a rejuvenated Eastern couldn't wait to divulge his hard earned findings. "Well overall I'm not sorry that you asked me for an opinion. I have to say that based on the evidence thus far, I strongly believe that what I've revealed from the content, is likely to prove to be 100% factual. I fear I may have jumped the gun a bit." Rogon, for his part, was quick to allay his sincerity.

"On the contrary Mike, you could well be forgiven for thinking otherwise, prior to your research. Having gone over the transcripts myself, I'm confident that our conclusions are on a parallel. My first instinct kept telling me that apart from anything else. Gleason's many omissions, although positive, retained a double edged meaning to them."

"Exactly my sentiments, the manner in which he explained himself on paper for instance, it was almost as if he was trying to tell us something. I refer to an example on occasion, of the written word 'our'. Is he stating 'our' as being the police as a whole, or could he be referring to a silent partnership? Likewise the constant use of two other words, 'he' and 'us' says to me that Gleason is talking collectively, and that in itself is dangerous."

"Precisely!" echoed Rogon. "Carrying on from that, what did you deduce from his parting shot, quote..."It takes a man to operate a car before it can become serviceable"...unquote."

"Bizarre, and I have to admit that one had me guessing for a while but working along the alleged partnership theory. I honestly think that the man he refers to is a leading associate, and that the car business, stupid as it may seem, consists of the conspirators including himself. In other words, you give the orders and we'll carry them out! That, in turn, begs the question, that just maybe your 'Mr Big' himself is still out there."

Having got his own view across, Rogon would have been happy just to allow the earth to swallow him up. "I have been dreading this moment Mike, knowing that you're nobody's fool and I suspect Gleason were he here would say likewise. As things stand, it's now beginning to look like we have inherited far more than we previously bargained for." Eastern meanwhile had alternative ideas. The expression 'beaten' didn't exist in his CV and for him, the show was still running.

"I beg to differ Rogon...the photos, there's something not quite kosher about them. On examination, I was reminded of our conversation yesterday when I implied that Gleason and Conway senior go back a long way...right? Including a stint in the army..." Stopping short he collected his thoughts. "By the way, from where did you manage to obtain these photos?"

"They were in the personal effects bag taken from Gleason's house...why do you ask?"

"And not Conway's?"

"No!" Spreading the four photos in question out on the table, Eastern pointed to them.

"In that case, take a good look at them again and tell me exactly what you see?" Shrugging his shoulders, Rogon carried out a quick analysis.

"Uhm...well apart from the one depicting Gleason and Travers together, the rest are all group scenes with them included."

"Right...anything else?" Eastern demanded. Rogon glanced upward in disbelief as hidden cogs co-joined positive wheels.

"I only assumed that because you stated the two had a history together. Working on that assumption, Conway would then become significant in the photos. In actual fact, his face doesn't show up at all in the other three?"

"Now you're thinking straight. Not only that, I can recall his daughter in law Joan Conway, nee Travers, informing me some time ago that he served exclusively in the Royal Navy...so, what does that tell you?" For the moment, Rogon had been left speechless as the last of the jigsaw finally fell into place. Then, and only then, was he available for comment.

"Travers?...Major bloody Travers, of course! It's all beginning to make sense now...'Mr Big' in person. It just beggars belief that a man of his standing managed to evade suspicion for so long. Right now, I'm having a problem dealing with the audacity of the man. I mean, what makes a man who's got everything, manic enough to want to throw it all away?"

Momentarily, Eastern found himself caught up in the heat of the moment, by allowing his subconscious to run off at a tangent and become surreal as the ghost of three blighted marriages entered the equation, forcing him into a private smile.

"Mike?"

"Oh sorry Rogon, I was somewhere else for a minute, but to get back to your question, yeah two probable reasons spring to mind."

"Which are?"

"Complete boredom in retirement, or the sheer buzz he generated, in knowing that he could just sit back and be in a position to manipulate the system, I guess."

"It would have made the perfect paradox if he's been allowed to get away with it. Have you any other thoughts on the matter Mike?" His question became lost in transit as Eastern deliberated.

"Only to say that what goes around…comes around. That sums it up for me Rogon, although knowing that the Major is in the frame doesn't make it any easier. I feel sorry for his family, the devious bastard has got a lot to answer for." Rogon nodded in a robotic manner then turned his attention toward the business in hand, as his mind shifted into spook modern.

"Well Mike, it's been a day to remember. From now on we can safely leave 'other business' in the hands of the IPCC. I would suggest that your time here with the agency, apart from a last debrief, has officially run its course. The bureaucracy of it all ends here I'm afraid, you know how it is?"

Eastern extended a token nod of sympathy that belied a hint of personal regret. "Only too well, once a spook always a spook, eh Rogon…?"

"And never out of sight, so don't you forget it Mike," he interrupted. Given time, Eastern might have cause to reflect on Rogon's prophesy. When you're ready I'll take you through for a debrief, but before we go this will be the last time we will be in a position to converse together. I just wanted to convey my thanks for your services Mike. You would make a great agency man, which reminds me, have you thought…"

Eastern had already accelerated the predictable offer and cut him short, "Another time, another place maybe, so thanks but no thanks... although..." He pondered briefly as he focused on a hidden agenda. "I need a favour...a big favour, it would mean a great deal to me personally, if it were made possible." During the next five minutes, the two discussed the logic and concerns surrounding his undisclosed plea, finally terminating with approval from both parties.

Thanking him once again, they warmly shook hands together, and said their respective goodbyes. Once outside the debriefing room, Rogon turned on his heel and didn't look back. Eastern watched him go until he disappeared from sight. His plastic figure inciting a thousand memories to flood back, and just as quickly fade into obscurity, except for one nagging doubt which seemed reluctant to let go.

"Why do I get the gut feeling, that this last meeting has the makings of a bleedin' dress rehearsal," he muttered to himself. In no time at all, he was blindfolded and escorted to an agency car, waiting to transport him back to Brighton and, what he believed to be, a whole new chapter in his life while embracing a world of reality, as he remembered it by.

Epilogue

A week or so after the media furore had subsided, Eastern would have readily admitted to you in confidence, "It became the hardest decision that I have ever had to make, especially at that moment in time, including the letter of course which explained my reasons for parting with Joan. As for the dreaded phone call to London, I realise now that in hindsight I could have handled the delicate situation a whole damn lot better. It was crass of me to allow the circumstances as a whole to take control of my selfish ego. Although at the time, I sincerely thought that it was the right thing to do.

Without due consideration, I seemed to have made Joan's mind up for her, mainly without any consultation as to her own feelings, towards the inevitable outcome her step father had unwittingly placed himself in. On the other hand, he alone chose the path that would culminate into his tragic death. And I make no excuses for the part that I played in his downfall. The complications arising with death of course can evoke a problem with the people you leave behind, and Joan is no exception. I can only hope that in time she will forgive me for playing 'Judas'. In my defence, it's fair to say that with or without me, I seriously believed that the Major would have taken the 'Gentleman's way out' anyway…but I digress.

The morning after splitting with the agency, I found myself going through the throes of a man in a hurry. Having placed a letter addressed to Joan in a convenient position, inside her flat in Brunswick Square. I shortly vacated the premises carrying a large suitcase, along with some various belongings which I placed in my car before heading off on an unrehearsed trip to Framfield, and an eagerly awaited confrontation with Major Travers.

A short distance away from my intended destination, I pulled into a service station and made a pre-planned mobile call. Glancing at my watch reminded me that I needed to be mindful regarding the absolute importance of my timing. Some fifteen minutes later I found myself parked up in the large courtyard, adjacent to the Travers residence. Having satisfied myself inwardly that my intentions were necessary, I alighted. Steeling myself, I rang the visitors' bell in the entrance area. Moments later Joan's mother appeared from behind the door.

"Mike? Good heavens!" She remarked, "What a welcome surprise, I must say you're the last person I expected to see...please come in. I know the Major will be pleased to see you, does Joan know you were calling in? I must ring her shortly."

For my part, there was no turning back now, and I couldn't afford to be blinded by courtesy. Rather I needed to alienate myself, by focusing on what I had set out to do. I quickly reassured Lady Travers that Joan was fine, and that I had conversed with her recently. I then asked her if I could possibly speak with the Major, "Business...you know how it is?" I explained to her in a pleasant manner.

Just then we were interrupted, "Who are you speaking to Celia? I heard voices and..." All of a sudden we were both greeted by the overly shocked looking Major.

"Well! Hello dear boy, if only I..." I didn't give him the satisfaction to finish and went straight for the proverbial jugular.

"We need to talk Sir, if that's acceptable? What I have to say shouldn't take long."

"But of course dear chap. I have to say that you have rather thrown me...what! Come on through, we can use my study." Shutting the door behind me, the Major ushered me toward a chair which I readily declined. As for the Major, he proceeded to make himself comfortable behind his desk. Glancing hurriedly at my watch reminded me that time was of the essence, knowing that an enforced conclusion to a third party deal was on the cards.

Without more ado I went for gold. "I think we can drop the old school tie routine Sir." I said. "I feel sure that the respect is mutual. I'd be very surprised if you didn't know why I am here." A look of sheer resignation masked the Major's face, and his breathing became erratic. I immediately sensed he was now aware that the road to perdition for him had finally run its course.

"It's all over...isn't it?" He spluttered and then resumed his verbal status quo. "I have been expecting you Mike, I can call you Mike? And now that you are here, I feel so much better...can you understand that?"

"Indeed!" I levelled with him. "But why...explain to me why did you do it to Joan of all people? And not forgetting Mrs Travers of course."

"Ah yes Joan, sorry about that old chap, I couldn't help myself. It wasn't the money don't you know. I say, you will take good care of her won't you? God! What have I done? I'm finished aren't I? There's so much I still need to do. Not that I haven't been prepared you understand. One has to be seen to be orderly, tacky is out of the question...what! I won't be seeing you again dear boy, although I'm sure you're aware of that anyway. I realise, exactly what I have to do to square things now."

The next minute he thrust his hand out for me to shake, more in desperation than in etiquette. Declining his offer, I shook my head before stating "I would have to be the worst type of hypocrite to accept that, you and I are worlds apart Major. And I happen to believe in the one that I live in. I'll see myself out...goodbye." Without more ado I exited the study and left the Major contemplating his immediate future.

"You will see Joan is alright, you did promise..." Was the last thing I heard him say as I closed the door behind me. Just then Lady Travers herself appeared.

"I'm off now madam, but hopefully I will be back in touch at some time. By the way, the Major told me to say that he didn't want to be disturbed for a while." Shaking her hand reverently, I then departed. I'd only just opened the door to my car, when the explicit blast from a shotgun coming from within the house, filled my ears. Unperturbed I drove off. Halfway down the gravel drive I passed two police squad cars heading towards the house. Glancing nonchalantly at my watch I smiled discreetly and said "Damn good timing that even for a spook, thanks Rogon, for everything."

In time, Henry Dowling was granted a posthumous Royal Pardon, and four other serving prisoners were in the process of having their respective cases reviewed. Cleared of all charges, assistant Chief Constable Conway decided to retire on medical grounds, and conveniently moved abroad to escape the hype surrounding his son. He is now currently servicing two life sentences and conspiracy charges.

As for me, I decided to move back to my old address and assume my flair as a PI. Two or three months went by and I received a phone call from Joan.

Consequently, we could be seen eating out together at a notable restaurant in the Lanes. For his part, Rogon continued to uphold the status quo, while secreted in a bubble of state security...I presume. Yeah, you could say that life for me is pretty good at the moment."

For the record and unbeknownst to Eastern, shortly after contacting the restaurant to secure his reservation. The call in question was intercepted and placed on file at spooks HQ for future monitoring.

The end......maybe?